A Special Life
Journey

Elisha White

ISBN 979-8-89526-264-1 (paperback)
ISBN 979-8-89526-265-8 (digital)

Christian Faith Publishing
832 Park Avenue
Meadville, PA 16335
www.christianfaithpublishing.com

Printed in the United States of America

1

Hate

"ELA! Where are you? Come here, love. BE A GOOD GIRL AND OBEY ME!" Vincent came into the run down apartment. I hid myself in the closet with a blanket. I couldn't handle being beaten or even sexually abused by him again.

I hated him, but I couldn't escape. He keeps everything locked, and he also keeps me in this room locked in with only an old, stained mattress on the floor and the blanket I cling to. He only feeds me a small loaf of bread every other day with a small glass of water.

He came stomping into the bedroom. I tried to make myself as small as possible as my body trembled. He flung open the closet door with a loud thud, and grabbed my long, strawberry-blonde hair and flung me on the bed.

He got on top of me, and I tried to fight him as much as I could, but he slapped my face and choked me. "You will obey your master. Now be a good girl and hold still," he said, as he choked me and sexually abused me till he was pleased.

"You should know by now, that you should obey me" he said, as he left the room and locked the door. I lay clutching myself on the bed, as I cried and my body trembled. I wanted to end it all, but couldn't bring myself to do it.

He was right from the beginning. I couldn't escape his hold on me. Ever since I was born, I was an orphan, and Vincent had control of me. He was twenty years older than me. I turned twenty one yesterday and he has been doing this to me for fifteen years.

1

I sobbed on that old, stained mattress for about an hour. Then I heard Vincent and his jerk friends scream something. I heard the door being unlocked, and Vincent came running in.

"Here, you can sell her. She will make a fine price with her body," he said as he grabbed my hair forcibly again and yanked me towards the tall men. They grabbed me and tied my wrist and ankles with ropes. They put the blanket around my body and dragged me out of the apartment. They put me in the trunk of a pitch-black car and shut it.

My body trembled, not just from the cold. I had no Idea what was about to wait for me, but I figured it wasn't going to be any better than what I was living in. I felt the car jerk as we began to move. I tried to untie my hands but it wasn't working.

I silently counted in my head each second that passed by. The smell in the trunk was so bad and it made my nose sting. The car moved for thirty minutes and forty five seconds, then it stopped and the engine was shut off.

They opened the trunk and stuck a bag over my head, to where I couldn't see. Someone picked me up and put me over their broad shoulder. They walked for about five minutes and slammed about five doors. I then heard keys jingling and they sat me on a very cold floor. They took the bag off my head, and I looked around.

I was in a dark cell in some kind of brick building. They locked the cell and walked out of the room. They then locked the door to the room. I tried to squirm and wiggle out of the ropes, but they were just too tight. I lay on my side and laid my head down on the cold, hard concrete floor.

I cried myself to sleep, just from the pain in my body. I woke up to the sun shining through the only window in the room. One of the people wearing a mask came in with a tray and something hanging on his arm.

"Rise and shine, beauty. We got to get you some clothes on and some food in your body. We also have to hide those scars and bruises on your body before we can sell you," he said, unlocking the cage and coming inside. He placed the stuff he had on the floor and helped me to sit up. He untied the ropes on my wrist and grabbed my wrist. He handcuffed one of my hands to one of the bars of the cage.

He tied what looked like a glittery bathing suit on me, then applied a concealer to the wounds on my body. He then spread a big blanket on the floor and sat down. I just stared at him, I didn't have the energy to say or do anything.

He picked up the tray of food and began feeding me pieces of a sandwich and chips. I took small bites as he fed me. He watched me as I ate each piece of food he handed me. After I was finished he gave me a cup of water, a hair brush, and a toothbrush and toothpaste.

I just looked at the items, not moving. He sighed and sat up on his knees and took the hair brush and brushed all the knots out of my hair. Then he brushed my teeth. He left carrying the tray after that making sure he locked the cage back up.

"Get some rest, sweet cakes. In about a week you will be going to an auction," he said.

I lay down on the blanket he left and wrapped it around my cold body. I stared at the wall and wondered if I was going to be sold to someone who actually was going to kill me, or if it would be someone like Vincent and his friends.

I continued to think of what the future was going to hold as I closed my eyes and drifted off to sleep. I woke up to two guys coming into the room and unlocking the cage. They were different from the man yesterday. They dropped the tray of food in front of me after they put the concealer on my body.

I ate the sandwich and chips and drank the water. Ten minutes later they came back and got the tray and locked the cage once again. I took the hair brush in my hand and looked at it for a while. Then I managed to pick up my arm halfway and brush through my hair.

I then sat up against the cold brick wall and stared outside the window. How nice it would be to be outside in that sunshine. I sighed and closed my eyes again. This little cycle reoccurred for four days.

2

The CEO

"Theo, are you going to the auction today?" Edna asked her grandson, as he got ready in his navy tuxedo suit.

"Yes, Grandma. I am going to get that valuable diamond necklace they have, for you no matter what it costs," Theo said, putting his shoes on and giving her a hug.

"Remember, God is with you in everything you do," she said,

"He will be good to us all. I will be back in a few hours. Don't do too much while I am away," he said, as he walked out of the door. He got in his 2025 Mustang and sped away to the auction. He prayed that he could get the valuable necklace.

What he didn't know is that God also had something planned that he would bring home. He arrived an hour later at the auction place. He parked and walked to the entrance and showed the invitation to the bouncer.

"Welcome Mr. Ambrose, we hope you enjoy" The bouncer said, bowing to Theo. Theo nodded and walked in. He got his fan number for the auction and went to go find his seat. He sat down at the table and ordered a cup of tea. He sipped on his tea for fifteen minutes then the spotlight shone on the stage and a man walked up.

"Welcome, ladies and gentlemen. We would like to personally welcome you to the black shadow auction. We have amazing treasures and artifacts for you all today. Bid the highest, and you will receive them. We have an even amazing piece at the end that is definitely worth everyone's while," the stage person said, giving a kind of evil laugh.

They started auctioning off different things from vases, to plates, to paintings. An hour passed and they brought out the magnificent, and highly valuable diamond stud necklace. The bid started at two thousand dollars. Theo raised his number. Then someone raised the bid higher to three thousand. Theo bid four thousand, and the other person bid five thousand.

The bid rose higher and higher. Going from seven thousand to eight to ten thousand. Theo continued to pray and bid as it steadily rose higher. Eventually, the final bid was fifteen thousand dollars, Theo raised his number and waited. The gavel went down on the pedestal. Theo won the bid.

The lights dimmed and the spot light shone on the stage again. "Ladies and gentlemen, now is the final event for the night. This isn't any object though. Our new highlight for the night is something far more valuable than any object. Tonight we have a rare natural beauty, named Ela," the person on stage said, as they brought out a fair-skinned, strawberry-blonde haired woman with emerald-green eyes, in a glittery bathing suit with a handkerchief tied in her mouth and her legs and arms tied. Theo's eyes met hers and everything around him felt like it froze.

'Theo, you need to save her. She is what you are here for.' Theo heard this. He questioned why God would want him to bid on her. As the bid started at a thousand dollars and rose quickly, God didn't leave much time for him to question it, as he started to bid on her.

He felt God's calling to save and protect her. He wasn't stupid; he knew when and how God spoke to him. He continued to bid until finally at ten thousand dollars, he won the bid on her. The gavel went down and it was official. People looked at him and gave him evil looks but it didn't faze him.

'God, I hope you know what you are doing. This is crazy.' Theo thought as he went to the back to collect the necklace and the girl. He trusted God, but he didn't know what God was planning. He collected the necklace and the girl.

He looked at the girl who was handcuffed and her mouth tied. He took his jacket off and wrapped it around her smaller body. He then picked her up bridal style and carried her to his Mustang. He placed her on the seat and closed her door.

He got in on the driver's side and turned towards her. "I don't know how you ended up here. I am not judging you whatsoever. I am not here to hurt you or take advantage of you. I want to help you. So I am going to untie you. I need you not to struggle, okay?"

He watched her, and he almost missed her, barely nodding. He first untied her mouth and dropped the handkerchief on the floor. Then he worked to untie her hands and feet. "Now, are you okay?" Theo asked, She nodded.

"Is there a place where I can take you, your home?" he asked, She shook her head no.

"Ok…um… so your name is Ela, right?" he asked, starting the engine. He looked at her and she nodded her head yes.

"Okay, my name is Theo. I am gonna take you to my house where my grandmother is, and she can help take a look at you to make sure you aren't hurt. Come now, let's buckle your seat belt," he said, as he reached over her to fasten her seat belt for her.

He started driving as she kept silent. He noticed she was slightly trembling as she looked down at her feet. Theo prayed for her. He didn't know what she had been through but he felt bad for her.

He drove to his condo house. He parked in the garage and shut the engine off. He looked at her and noticed she had fallen asleep. He unbuckled her seat belt and carried her into the house.

"Theo, who is this? What is going on? What happened?" Edna asked as he brought her into the living room. He went up the steps as Edna waited in the living room. He gently placed Ela in the Guest bed of the guest bedroom and shut the door. He went back down and sat beside Edna.

"Before you freak out, she was being sold at the auction and God told me I needed to save her. I don't know what his plan is, but she looked like she was scared and had been through a lot of trauma. She told me she had nowhere to go and no home to go to. She also said she didn't have any family. I want to help her as much as I can.

Do you know what size clothes she would be able to wear?" Theo said, handing Edna the necklace.

"From what I could tell, small or medium. Did she tell you anything more than that?" Edna asked looking up the stairs.

"No, she didn't speak at all. She answered my questions by just nodding her head. I don't know what her voice sounds like. Can I ask you to go with Assistant Scott and get her some clothes? She also looks malnourished, so might need to get some vitamins as well," he said, running his fingers through his dark brown hair.

"Okay, I am sure God has a plan. Do you need me to get her anything else?" Edna said, standing up.

"Yeah, when she wakes up can you check her to make sure she isn't hurt anywhere? It would be nice to ease my mind and think she wasn't beat, but I am not too sure," he said, putting his phone away.

"Yeah, I can. Is Assistant Scott outside?" she asked.

"Yeah," he said.

"Don't worry, It is going to be okay," she said, heading out the door.

3

New Life?

I woke up in a soft, comfortable, and warm bed. I took the covers off of myself and noticed I was wearing sweatpants and a sweatshirt. I sat up and tried to remember the past few days. Bits and pieces of my memory tried to come back but a lot of it was fuzzy. Just as I was about to get up, there was a knock on the door. An older woman came into the room with a tray.

"Oh, good, you are awake. Here you go, dear, this should help you regain strength and heal your body," the older woman said, as she laid the tray on my lap. There was a bowl of some really good smelling soup, and some little triangle sandwiches, and a little tea cup with some good smelling tea in it.

"My name is Edna, dear, don't worry about a thing while you are here. We will take care of you. I bought you some different clothes to wear. They are in the closet over there. My grandson, Theo, will be here in a little bit to talk to you some more," she said, pointing then exiting the room.

I began to eat the food. It warmed my body up and made me feel like I was getting energy again. I finished everything on the tray, and placed it on the table beside the bed. As I did there was a knock on my door, I looked up to see Theo standing in the doorway.

"Hey, how are you feeling? I am glad you are up. Would you like to come down to the living room?" he asked, I nodded. I placed my feet on the floor and winced in pain.

"Yeah, you have some cuts and stuff on the bottom of your feet. I guess you got them from the auction. Here let me help you to the living room," he said, picking me up in his arms and carrying me down the stairs and gently placing me on the couch.

He sat next to me, and I could smell a strong scent coming off of him. "I don't know what you have been through and I honestly don't know if I can help you, but I want to try, God has a plan for you being here, I just don't know what" he said.

I gave him a questioning look, and he made a face like he understood why I was confused. He stood up and grabbed a leather book that had the words "Holy Bible" on it. He brought it close to me and put it in my lap.

He started to explain who God was and what a Christian was. He explained what they believe in. He showed me the verses of the Bible and explained it. He then got a phone call, and I kept trying to read on my own but got quickly confused.

So I watched him talk on the phone instead. I don't know what it was about him, but it made me feel like I could trust him, and he would be kind to me. He hung up the phone and turned around and saw me watching him.

He smiled and came back to the couch. He continued to explain the Bible to me and something in my heart changed in me. I knew I was lost and a sinner, so I asked God to come into my heart and save me. He noticed and said "You just got saved, didn't you?"

I was having feelings I didn't know existed before. I nodded, feeling excited and overwhelmed and scared at the same time. He helped explain a little more and we kept studying. We studied so late that we didn't even realize we fell asleep on the couch.

We woke up the next morning, and looked around confused. We looked at each other, and he laughed. He got up off the couch and into the kitchen. I put on some house shoes Edna brought in yesterday.

I went upstairs and took a shower. It was nice to have independence and be able to take showers again. I put on some skin care that Edna showed me how to use. I went down stairs and sat at the table.

Theo came to the table and placed a plate of eggs, bacon and fruit in front of me. He sat down with his plate across from me. He started to say, what he called, the blessing over the food. Then we began to eat the food.

My body shivered in anticipation as the first taste of this amazing food hit my taste buds. I made a happy face, as I wasn't used to eating delicious food like this. Theo looked up and chuckled.

"I take it, you weren't fed well where you came from huh?" he asked. I shook my head no.

"Were you taught anything? Like reading or writing?" he asked, taking a bite of scrambled eggs. I shook my head and made a "kind of" motion with my hand.

"I will teach you. Grandma can help you get into some business appropriate attire and you can go to my company. I will help you learn all you need to know," Theo said, finishing his coffee and taking his dishes to the sink.

I finished my last bite and followed him, I put away the dishes and followed Edna up the stairs. She went to my closet and pulled out what she called a blouse and a skirt. I got changed, and she showed me how to put on a little mascara.

She then gave me some shoes, which she called flats. I put them on and looked at myself in the mirror. I didn't look bad, She told me I looked elegant and sophisticated. She then handed me a bottle of a pinkish liquid. I gave her a puzzled look.

"It is perfume, dear. You spray a little bit on your neck and wrist to make you smell good. Like this" Edna said, as she sprayed the stuff on my neck and wrist. "Now rub your wrist together," she said, I did.

We then went out of the room and down the stairs. When I made it halfway down the stairs I looked up and saw Theo in a suit looking at me. We stared at each for a good while before I made it down the stairs to his side.

4

Teaching Her the Basics

Theo got dressed and waited for Ela at the bottom of the stairs. He heard the guest bedroom door shut and looked up. He started to stare at her as she made her way down the clear stairs.

'*Wow, she looks beautiful. Wait, no, I can't be attracted to her. She needs my help, nothing else. God help me to not push the boundaries too far. Give me strength Lord.*' Theo thought as she made her way to his side.

"Are you ready to go?" he asked, She nodded and they walked out of the house. He opened the passenger side door of a Rolls Royce for her. She climbed in and he shut the door.

He got in on the driver side door and he saw she buckled her own seat belt. He started the car and backed out of the garage and into the street. He drove thirty minutes to his company and parked in the CEO parking spot.

He got out, opened the door for Ela, and helped her out. She looked around, looking a tad over whelmed. He took her hand in his and said "It is okay, I am here with you. Don't worry."

He led her to an elevator and pushed the top number. They rode in the elevator for a little bit, till there was a little *ding*. Ela jumped and clung to his arm.

"It is okay. It is just the elevator saying we arrived on the floor. Come on" he said, taking her hand and guiding her in the office. They made their way past Assistant Scott who greeted them good morning.

He led her into his office and shut the door. "You can sit on the couch. Once I go through my emails I will start teaching you how to write, okay?" he said, as he went to his desk.

He sat down and started to type on his double-screen computer. It took him thirty minutes to go through all the emails. Then he got a notepad and a Pen from his desk and made his way to Ela.

He sat down and started to teach. He taught her basic words and how to write and use them in a sentence. At ten thirty, a knock came from the door, Theo said to come in and Assistant Scott walked in.

"Sir, the company we are wanting to collaborate with is here for the meeting," Assistant Scott said, bowing.

"Thank you, I am heading there now," Theo told his assistant, then turned towards Ela. "I have to go to a meeting, keep practicing what I have taught you so far. Once I am done with the meeting, we will go for lunch," he said, she nodded and got back to work.

He rose from the couch in his office and made his way out and went inside the elevator. He pressed the number 8 button and waited for the elevator to get there. He stepped out of the elevator and made his way to the meeting room.

When he went inside, he held out his hand to Mr. Norman. The person from the other company. "Mr. Norman, a pleasure to have you here. Are you ready to start the meeting?" Theo asked, as they shook hands.

"Yes, please," Mr. Norman said, in a thick accent.

They began their meeting, going over gains and losses, market values, and benefits. The meeting took an hour and thirty minutes. They shook hands and Assistant Scott showed them out.

Theo went back into the elevator and hit the number 10 button. The elevator dinged, and he stepped out. He went into the office and saw Ela working hard, trying to write the things he taught her. He smiled and walked closer to her.

She looked up at him and smiled, holding up the work she did, for him to see. "Good job, that is great! You are a fast learner. Are you ready to go eat lunch?"

She nodded and sat the work on the coffee table. She stood and took his outstretched hand. They made their way to the elevator and pressed the G button. They went into the parking garage and got in the car.

Theo drove to a fancy restaurant and parked. He opened the door for Ela and helped her out. They made their way inside and a waitress led them to a VIP table. She gave them menus and walked to get their drinks.

"Point to whatever you want. There is no limit," he said, and she nodded, looking over the menu. A few minutes later, the waitress came back with their drinks and asked if they were ready to order.

"I will have the six ounce sirloin, with a sweet potato and side salad. Ela, what do you want?" he asked. She put her menu down and pointed at a picture and showed him. "She wants the six ounce ribeye with sweet potato fries and a side salad," he said, handing the menus to the waitress.

"You will love it. Their food is incredible," he said, she nodded and smiled. The food came fifteen minutes later, and they began eating. Ela took a bite and gave a little face of satisfaction. Theo chuckled again.

"I told you they had amazing food," Theo said.

They ate their food and drank their tea. They finished up and Theo got the bill. He gave his black card to the waitress and she ran it. He got his card back and they exited the restaurant.

He drove back to the company and went back into his office. He showed Ela how to do basic math and form simple sentences with the words she just learned. He then began to work on signing contracts and other things. The clock hit four o' clock, and he shut down his computer and walked towards Ela.

"Are you ready to go back home?" he asked her, She nodded and cleaned up her work. They left the company and headed back to his house.

5

True Happiness?

I don't know how or why, but I feel so happy with Theo. He taught me so much today. I finally feel free. I thought to myself, as I stared out the window of his car as he drove to his house.

We made it home and went inside. Edna was in the kitchen and called me over to her. "I am going to teach you how to cook. So put this on," she said, handing me an apron. "First I am going to teach you how to chop vegetables," she said, showing me how to chop all the different types of vegetables.

Then she showed me how to cook the vegetables with the meat. I followed her instructions as she gave them to me. Then she showed me how to set the table with the cooked food.

Theo came down and saw I had done the cooking. He smiled and sat at the table. We sat down and held hands as we blessed the food. We ate the stir fry and cleaned up. Theo went out for a bit, so I went to the study to see if I could find any books that could help me, to surprise him.

I found some books about etiquette and speech and different things and began to read. I took notes on different things. I worked hard to learn all the etiquette in my room. I heard the door open and close, so I finished the book and went down the stairs. I couldn't find Theo so I went to the study room.

I saw he was at his desk in the study and quietly walked in. Then I stood up tall and finally got the courage to speak. "T…Theo?" I said. He jerked his head up and his eyes went wide.

"You … you spoke," he said, looking surprised. I nodded, as he stood up from his desk and made his way to me.

"Say it again. Say my name," He looked at me with a begging look.

"Th…Theo," I said a little louder. He chuckled and picked me up and spun me in his arms. I giggled as he sat me back down.

"This is great. I finally get to hear how your voice sounds. It's beautiful," he said, smiling.

"Th-thank… you," I said, his face looking surprised again.

"Did you need something?" He asked.

"H-help… y…you" I managed to say, looking in his hazel eyes.

"You wanted to help me?" he said, smiling. I nodded. "You can say it"

"y-yes," I said, looking down.

"Good job, you did good," he said, petting my head. "Come on, I will show you what I am working on."

He guided me to his desk. He pulled up another chair beside him, and I sat beside him. He showed me the building he was trying to get and trying to figure out what to do with it.

"What do you think I should do with it?" he asked, looking at me.

"A-animal" I said, he looked a little confused.

"Animal?" He asked, I nodded, got up and grabbed the picture I found of an animal adoption center.

"A-animal" I said, pointing to the building in the photo.

"Oh, an animal adoption center, I see," he said, and I nodded quickly.

"I could do that. Let people surrender animals they can't take care of anymore and have someone find them good homes," he said, putting a finger to his lips.

"M-me" I said. He looked at me

"What about you?" He asked, watching my movements.

"B-building," I said, pointing at the screen.

"You want to run it?" He asked, his eyes getting bigger. I nodded quickly and said, "Y-yes"

"Are you sure? Taking care of a building is hard work, much less taking care of animals," he said.

"R-run …it," I said, nodding.

"Okay, but before we do that, you are going to have to learn some more things before you can run it. Are you up for the challenge?" he asked, taking my hand.

"Y-yes" I said, squeezing his hand, looking in his eyes again.

"Alright, then let's get started," he said, as he stood up and got some books and folders out of the bookshelf. He started to teach me how to run a business and keep it maintained and clean. He gave me a book all about animals.

"Tomorrow, I will take you to meet an abused horse and let you get some experience with handling animals," he said, stacking the books we used.

"O-ok" I said, nodding.

"Go get some rest, it is late," he said, I nodded and stood up and walked to the door.

"Go-.good …n-.night," I said, turning to him then going upstairs.

I got ready for bed and laid down. I felt excited and determined to impress him and help those animals. I stared at the ceiling for a little bit, then drifted off to sleep. I woke up the next morning and jumped out of bed. I braided my hair and ran down the stairs.

"Whoa, you're excited for today huh?" Theo asked me, as I collided into him.

"Y-yes" I smiled, looking into his eyes.

"Well then let's go," he said, chuckling.

We made it to the field and we walked to the pasture the abused horse was in. "I will be right here beside you. If the horse rears up on its hind legs, you turn and run, okay?" he said.

"O-okay" I nodded. He helped me climb the fence. Once my feet hit the ground I started to talk to God in my head. '*God, I want to help this poor animal like you and Theo helped me. Help me to connect to it and for it to trust me.*'

I slowly stepped closer to the horse: its body was trembling. I stopped in the middle of the pasture and put my hand out. I spoke softly to it. "C-come…i-it …i-is…o-okay." It stared at me for a little bit. I said again, "O-okay". It slowly started to walk towards me.

When it got close, I stayed still letting it choose what it wanted to do. I kept my hand out and it smelled my hand. A few minutes passed by, then it put its nose under my hand and came a little closer to where my arm bent and my face was close to the horse's face.

I lowered my forehead to its face and said "I…kn-know … you." then started to pet its muzzle with my other hand and said, "G-good." I slowly started to walk to the side of it and started to pet its neck. I then let go of it and started to walk slowly to where the supplies were.

It followed me, I held its head and picked up the curry comb. I showed it to it and let it sniff it. I told it "I-It … is …o-ok … w-won't … h-hurt…y-you" Then I started to comb it's fur. It's body shook, but it let me do it. I went gentle and slow with brushing it so as to not spook it. I looked at Theo and he looked shocked and happy at the same time. I then wet a rag, did the same process, and wiped the dirt off of its body. Then I brushed through its mane and braided its mane. I then fed it some carrots Theo had brought with him.

I put my hand under its chin and said "C-come." It started to follow me, and we walked the perimeter of the pasture. I looked at Theo and noticed he was filming me, I smiled at him and continued to walk with the horse.

I fed it more carrots then started to walk towards Theo. He asked if I enjoyed helping the horse while helping me to climb the fence. "Y-yes," I said, as the tennis shoes I was wearing hit the ground.

"B-bring … t-to… b-building?" I asked, looking at him as we walked to the car.

"Yeah, we can bring it to the building. There is a grassy area behind the building we can bring it to once we get a fence made for it and work on the building," he said, as he opened my door.

"L-lets …g-go …d-do …i-it" I said, as I climbed in and he shut the door. We went to a place called tractor supply and got all the stuff we needed. We began working on the outside of the building first. We made the fence for the horse, a little shed and put hay in the shed.

We painted the outside walls of the building. Then unlocked the doors and went inside and started to make habitats for different animals that would be coming in. stocked shelves with different animal feed.

Then there was a knock at the door, with a man delivering a sign that when we unboxed it, it said "Ela's animal adoption and rehab center". Theo and his assistant got ladders and hung up the sign at the front.

They then put up the open sign on the window. Then at the end of the day we went back home. Each day for three weeks, I learned how to take care of different animals and how to take care of a building.

The first day I was about to open, Theo dropped me off and asked me "Are you ready for your first day?"

"I am. I am … glad we got the …horse moved over… to the building," I said. My speaking was getting better, but not to the level of Theo's speaking.

"Yeah, you are gonna do great. I will pick you up this afternoon," he said, giving my hand a squeeze.

"Ok," I said and got out of the car. I went to unlock the door and noticed a box in front of the double doors. I unlocked the doors and bent down and picked up the box and took it inside. I turned the lights on and turned the open sign on. I took the box to the back room where the rehab enclosures are and looked inside the box.

There was a very skinny bearded dragon and a piece of paper in the box. I opened the piece of paper and read *"I can't take care of this thing anymore. I can't keep feeding it disgusting bugs. Ugh."* I rolled my eyes and picked up the little guy.

I looked him over and made sure nothing else was wrong with him. Then I fixed him a little container with a warm damp paper towel to get him some humidity, while I made his rehab enclosure. I then got a small meal worm from the feed containers and offered it to the bearded dragon.

He took it right away and then I put him in the rehab enclosure. Once he got back to being healthy, I could put him out front to be adopted. We already had a few animals that we got from shelters to be adopted.

I then started to prepare all the animals' food for the day. A mealworm for Cici, the leopard gecko. Pellets for Tyrone, the hamster. Kitten food for Ginger, the kitten. Then I went to the back to give brownie, the horse, some grain.

I started to check emails on the computer Theo set up for me. I was told the other day that someone is going to bring a bird to the center today, because they couldn't keep it because they were moving.

I cleaned the place up and waited. Then the doorbell rang. "Welcome," I said, looking at the door. They came to the door and put the bird and cage on the counter. "Thank you so much again for taking her." they said, looking relieved. "No… problem," I said, they waved goodbye and said her name was charlotte.

"Hello… Charlotte… Let us …put you in … A bigger cage." I said, and let her climb on my fingers so she could get out of that small cage. I put her in the bigger bird cage I had on the wall.

She started to fly around the cage, enjoying the bigger one. I put the smaller cage in the back. I put some pellets for Charlotte in her cage. I refilled water bottles and dishes. I kept stocking shelves with food, hides, water and food dishes, fake plants, cages for sale, sand, rocks, and other things.

A few people came in and looked around, and left after buying stuff they needed. None of the animals have been adopted yet. Lunch time came around and Assistant Scott brought me some food. I ate it and went back to work.

A few hours went by and a person came in carrying a large box. "Welcome," I said.

"Hey, I heard you take in animals that people can't take care of anymore. Is that right?" The person said.

"I …do," I said, as she placed the big box on the counter. She pushed the box and left before I could do or say anything more. I looked in the box and saw deli containers full of reptiles.

I pulled the first container out, it was a hognose snake which looked like it had stuck shed on it. The next container had a banana ball python, which looked like it was starving. The last container had a crested gecko, which looked fine.

I took each of the reptiles to the back and looked over them well. I put the hognose in a warm damp container that was placed under a heat lamp, to help soften the stuck shed. I made an enclosure for the ball python and before I put it in I offered it a thawed out mouse.

It took it without any problems. I let it swallow the mouse while I checked the gecko, then took the gecko to the adoption enclosures in the front for it to be adopted. I gave it a water dish full of water and a small meal worm.

I went back to the python, saw it had swallowed the mouse, picked it up and put it into a rehab enclosure. Gave the enclosure a little moisture with a spray bottle and filled the water dish. I closed and locked the doors to the enclosure.

I walked over to the hognose after the forty minutes passed and saw it was still trying to get the shed off. I got a pair of tweezers and helped get all of the shed off. Once that was done, I looked it over again to make sure there wasn't anything more wrong with it. I then put it in an empty container and fed it a little thawed pinky mouse. It took it, no problem and once it finished I carried it to an adoption enclosure and gave it a water dish with water and moistened the substrate.

I made sure every occupied enclosure had a water dish and made sure they had eaten. Then I made sure all enclosures were locked, so that nothing could escape. I cut the open sign off and locked the front doors.

I made my way to the back to take brownie the horse to the shed that was built into the fenced in area. Gave him hay for the night and filled his water bucket up. I went back inside and cleaned up while I waited for Theo to come.

He pulled in the parking lot and I walked to the door and unlocked it and let him in. He came in and closed and locked the door behind him. He went to go look at all of the animals that had been surrendered.

"Did you have a good day? Did you receive any little ones that had to be rehabbed," he asked, tapping the glass of the hognose snake.

"Yes... to ...both," I said, grabbing his hand and taking him to the back. I showed him the bearded dragon, the gecko, and the ball python. He looked at them all and smiled.

"You will take care of them, and get them back to health. I just know it," he said. We started to cut all of the lights off and went to the car. Making sure the doors were locked, we got in the car.

"There is something I wanted to ask you. There is a formal party the company is hosting, and I was wondering if you would be my partner?" He asked, looking nervous.

"Yes," I said, looking at him.

"Really, you would want to go with me?" He looked at me for a moment then back at the road. I nodded, as we turned into town.

"Then let's get some clothes to wear to it," he said, as we pulled into the mall parking lot. We walked in and saw many stores. We walked into a formal store and started looking around. I found a gorgeous, black sparkly, off the shoulder, princess style dress and went to try it on.

I came out of the dressing room and went to the stage with the mirror. Theo walked in, with a black suit on and stared.

"Does... it... look...good?" I asked, meeting his eyes in the mirror.

"Yes, looks perfect, absolutely stunning," he said walking on the stage "Now, I want you to practice walking with me in this dress, think you can do that?" He asked, holding his elbow out.

I remembered reading in a book, that when they do that, I am supposed to take his arm with my hand, and walk with him as he guides me. I did that and we started to walk off the stage and around the store.

We then stopped after doing that for about thirty minutes and got dressed back into our other clothes. We took our outfits and brought them to the checkout counter. The lady took them and wrapped them and Theo paid for them. We then went home, ate supper and got ready for bed.

6

Getting through the Week

Theo was so mesmerized by how Ela looked so radiant and sophisticated and just beautiful in that formal dress. He went to bed thinking about dancing with her at the party Friday. He just had to make it through three more days, then get ready that afternoon.

Lord, I am not sure what your plan is for me and Ela. I pray that everything goes well and she continues to love and learn more about you. I pray that she continues to enjoy church. Lord help me to protect her. I want to always help her to the best of my ability. Lord she is absolutely amazing. I want to keep helping her grow and learn.

He kept talking to God as he fell asleep. The next morning, he woke up and got dressed for work. He went downstairs to where Edna was making breakfast and sat at the table with his Bible and morning journal.

Ela came down, and sat beside him, they ate while they did their morning study. They read the first two chapters of the book of Acts and finished eating. Then they got their bags and went to the garage.

They both got in and Theo drove Ela to her building, told her that he would pick her up for lunch, then left for the company. He arrived thirty minutes later and parked in his CEO spot. He got out and went to the elevator that takes him to his office.

He made it in, said good morning to his assistant and sat at his desk. He started the day by checking his emails. Then got to work signing documents, looking over the spreadsheets for the markets, and answering emails.

He told his assistant to make a meeting with the sales team this afternoon. He then made a powerpoint of all the gains and losses for the company. When he was done it was eleven thirty.

He told his assistant he was going to grab Ela and go for lunch. The assistant agreed and took over for Theo. He went down the elevator and got in his Bugatti. He headed towards Ela's building.

He arrived at her parking lot and went inside. He saw there was a puppy that had gotten surrendered. He pet the puppy and kitten then went to the back to find Ela. He made his way behind the counter and opened the door that led to the back.

He saw Ela feeding a baby sugar glider, holding onto a stuffed bear. She looked up and smiled. He went and stood beside her and pet the little one. "Are you almost ready to go?" He asked.

"Yeah…just let… this little one finish eating… and I will put it in the rehab enclosure …I made for it," Ela said, as the little one finished the last drop of the bottle. Theo watched her as she put the little one in an enclosure she had made for it.

She then came to his side and smiled. He grabbed her hand and brought her out of the back. She grabbed the out for lunch sign and stuck it on the door, then turned the open sign off. He grabbed her hand again and they exited the building. She locked the door and they headed for lunch.

He drove her to a kind of fast food restaurant and they ordered mozzarella sticks, fried pickles, and catfish. They got the food and began eating. Theo then got the courage to start a conversation.

"Are people buying anything at the building?" he asked, taking a bite of the mozzarella stick.

"Yes… sold some… food … And hides… and the hamster," she said, as she ate some of the fried pickles.

"That's good, hopefully you can keep getting the animals adopted," he said, she nodded and took another bite of catfish.

They talked and ate for a while then headed back to the car. He dropped her off and told her to wait for him to pick her up, then left to go back to the company. He arrived at his company and went inside the elevator.

He went inside his office and got his materials ready for the afternoon meeting. He then went down with his assistant to the eighth floor and went into the meeting room. They started the meeting and went over everything about the sales of the company.

The meeting lasted two hours and was dismissed. Theo went back to his office and worked on more contracts and documents. He did that for an hour. When four o'clock hit, he stacked up everything and went to the elevator.

He got in his Bugatti and went to pick Ela up. He drove thirty minutes and arrived in her parking lot. He saw the open sign off so he used his key to get in. He looked at all the animals, before making his way to the back.

He saw Ela refilling water dishes in the rehab enclosures. "How was your day?" He asked, leaning on the door frame, watching her.

"Good," she said, looking at him for a moment, then finishing what she was doing. She started to write on her paper that was on the clipboard. Then she went to the front and logged out of the computer. She grabbed his hand and guided him to the entrance with a smile.

He smiled back and let her do it. They went outside and she locked the door. He offered her his hand and she took it. He guided her to his Bugatti and opened her door. She got in and he got in on the driver's side.

He drove them home and helped her out. They went into the condo house and saw a note on the kitchen counter. They both read the note:

"I am going out with some friends of mine, don't worry about me, there are some leftovers in the fridge -Edna"

Theo smiled and shook his head. He went to the fridge and saw the leftovers in a container. He got it out and heated it up. He placed it on the table and they blessed their food and began eating. Once they were done they cleaned up the kitchen and went to the living room.

Theo got his Bible and his and Ela's journal. They did their evening Bible study and lesson and talked about what they studied. Then as it turned eight thirty, they put their stuff away and went to get ready for bed.

7

The Past Can Haunt You

I woke up the next morning, and got ready for work. I was excited for tomorrow afternoon, but still had my responsibilities. I finished getting ready, and went downstairs. I ate some eggs on toast. Then we went to the garage to get into Theo's Lamborghini.

We talked as we rode to my building. When we arrived we saw some posters taped to the building and windows. Theo parked and we got out of the vehicle. As we got closer, we saw that it was a picture of me from my past, with bad words written on them.

I started to panic and hyperventilate. Theo noticed and pulled me into his arms and made shushing noises in my ear. I calmed down, while listening to his heartbeat. He let me go and told me to go inside. I obeyed and opened the door and cut the lights on.

I watched him as he took all the posters down and shoved them together and threw them in the trash. He then came in and walked towards me. He looked me in the eyes and said, "Are you okay? If you don't feel safe I will stay here with you."

"I am… Okay," I said, sighing and looking down. He moved his right hand and gently pushed my chin up so that I was looking at his eyes.

"If you want me to stay here and protect you I will. I have my laptop so I can work from here. Just say the word and I will stay," he said, with a determined look searching my face.

"Please… stay," I felt guilty making him stay with me, but if Vincent did this, he could try to come back and kidnap me or worse kill me. Theo pulled me into his arms as he saw me shaking. He comforted me till I calmed down, then went to his car and got his bag out and brought it in.

I started my work day as he sat at the counter, working while keeping an eye on me. I began by feeding all the animals that were to be fed that day. I then refilled each water dish and checked on the rehab animals.

I started to clean each enclosure and went to Theo's side to check the emails. Theo smiled at me while giving my hand a squeeze, then continued to talk on the phone. I noticed an email saying,

"I have a koi fish that has gotten too big for me to take care of now, Can you help me?"

I replied to the email, saying to bring it over. I went to the back to make sure the turtle pond they had built in a spare room was able to fit a koi. It was, so I made sure the temperature was fine and the live plants were still thriving. The pond had a cave system that went to the small pond in the pasture.

Theo had let brownie out in the pasture that morning and fed him. I went back out front and saw the man was bringing the koi fish in from the parking lot. I put on some gloves and welcomed him as he handed me the tank with the koi fish. I thanked him and brought the fish to the back.

I looked over the fish to make sure nothing was wrong with it, while keeping it in the tank. Then got some of the water out of the tank into a large enough container for it. Then I put the fish in the container. I tied the container to the edge of the turtle pond in the room so that the fish could acclimate to the water.

After about thirty minutes I turned the container slightly and the fish swam into the pond. I gave it some fish food and watched it eat. It swam into the cave system after it finished eating and I went back out front.

When I went into the front room I saw Theo typing on his computer. I smiled and let the puppy and kitten out of their cages to get some exercise. I put a harness on the puppy and walked and trained it.

I gave both of them treats when they did well. I got their toys and started to play with them. Once they lay down and looked tired I picked them up and put them back in their kennels.

At that time a few customers walked in, they were looking for a small pet for their son. I guided them over to the adoption part of the building and showed them the gecko. They said they wanted something a little fluffier, so I guided them to the kitten.

I took it out of the kennel, and let them hold it and play with it. They were happy with it and said they would adopt it. I guided them to the counter and printed the adoption paperwork for them to fill out.

I packed their goody bags of the basics for the kitten while they were filling out the paperwork and placed the bag on the counter. They handed me the paperwork and I entered all of their information. Of course I did background checks while they did the paperwork.

Once everything was entered, they were good to go. They put the kitten in the travel box with my logo on it and went to their car. I cleaned out the kennel that the kitten was in. I took the litter box and bed out, and stuck the bed in the small washing machine in the back. Then I took out the bowls and gave them a wash in the double sink, in the back. I sprayed a sanitizer in the kennel and wiped it clean. I closed the kennel and brought the cleaning supplies back in the back. The phone rang. As I went to the front to answer it, Theo grabbed it and answered it.

"Ela's Adoption and Rehab Center, this is Theo. How may I help you?" he said, looking and smiling at me. "So you have a turtle that was attacked by a dog, and a baby ferret that you can't take care of?" He asked, writing the details down.

"Okay, I got it, you can bring them over as soon as you can." He handed me the sheet he wrote the information on and I printed off the pages where I could put the information and examine the extent of the injuries. I emailed the vet, to be on standby in case the injuries of the turtle were servere.

A woman came in with a box, and sat it on the counter. She thanked us for taking them and left. I took them to the back and set up everything. I started with the ferret. I got the weight of it and checked its body for any wounds. I checked it eyes and mouth to make sure nothing was wrong there. I sat it on the metal table and got an egg from the fridge.

I offered it the egg. It sniffed the raw egg on the plate then started to eat it. I let it finish then put it in a temporary container till I could get the adoption enclosure ready. I got the container that had the turtle in it, out of the box.

I started by weighing it, it was a normal weight. The shell was slightly cracked and some blood was coming out. I told Theo to ask the vet to come and bring the portable x-ray to see if there was any internal damage. I put it back in the container it came in and grabbed the supplies to make the enclosure for the ferret. I put some bedding down and Gave it a hide, a toy and a water and food dish. I filled the water dish and put some pellets in the food dish.

I then brought the ferret out and put it in the adoption enclosure. I closed the door to the enclosure and locked it. I watched it play with the toy before I went back to the back and started to create the rehab enclosure for the turtle. I put in coco husk substrate and put a hide and the two dishes. I gave it a piece of tree bark in the corner of the enclosure.

The vet had arrived then, Theo told her to come to the back. She examined the turtle and took an x-ray. There was no internal damage, just the shell. So we patched the shell up and wrapped it with an adhesive bandage.

I put the turtle in the enclosure and gave it some turtle food in the dish. I thanked the vet and shook her hand as she left. I followed her back to the front and made sure all the enclosures were clean.

Then I swept the floor and put all the information on the two new animals in the computer. It was now lunch time and a delivery man came in and handed Theo some food. Theo paid him in cash and he left.

He spread the food on the back counter, and we began to eat the tacos and nachos. We talked for a while and when I turned to the door to welcome the customer that walked in, I saw it was Malcom. My heart dropped, and my smile turned into a frown. Theo noticed and looked at the door. He held my hand to calm my shaking and whispered to me.

"Is that one of the people who hurt you in the past?" Theo asked, as Malcom came closer to the counter. I nodded and got closer to the side of Theo. He held my hand tighter and stood up.

"Malcom,… what are… You doing… here" I asked, trying to stay calm, as he reached the counter.

"You can talk?" He asked, surprised with a look of shock on his face.

"Yes" I said, tightening my grip on Theo's hand to keep from shaking.

"Right…um I just wanted to see if this was your store… And I wanted to come and talk to you," he said, moving nervously.

"Yes, it is… why do you… want to talk?" I said, as Theo watched us, while keeping his hand on mine.

"Well, can we talk in private?" He asked, looking over at Theo then at our hands.

"No, you can speak to her in front of me. I am here to protect her, and to be honest I don't trust you being alone with her." Theo said, stepping closer. I smiled at him and nodded.

"I just wanted to talk to you and say, I am sorry for the past, how Vincent treated you and how I acted. I wanted to ask if you will come back home. We will treat you better, I promise." Malcom said, I trembled as he said Vincent's name. Theo scoffed and wrapped his arm around my shoulders.

"No," I said, looking down as I couldn't face him. I leaned closer to Theo.

"Come on, we promise to do better. Come back home with me." He kept insisting. I shook my head and buried it in Theo's broad shoulder.

"she said no, now get out of here before I call the cops for what you did to her in the past." Theo said, a stern look on his face as he hugged me to calm my trembling. Malcom was shocked, then turned and walked out of the store.

"Shhhh, It's okay now, I am here and he is gone," Theo said, as my body trembled in his grasp. I hugged him as tight as I could and tried to calm my breathing down while I listened to his heart. It took about fifteen minutes, he let me go and started to talk.

"I am going to lock the door and turn the sign off, then I want you to tell me everything they have done to you and who it all was. They will get the punishment they deserve," he said, as he walked to the front door and locked it and shut the sign off. He grabbed my hand and sat me down beside him. "Okay, now I need to know. Don't be scared because I am right here."

8

Learning Her Past and Protecting Her

Theo held her hand and looked at her as she began to speak about her past. He took his jacket off and wrapped it around her to make her feel more comfortable. He felt her tremble as she started to talk about it.

"I was an orphan since I was born… and since I can remember, Vincent and his friends … have been the only people I had known… I trusted them…but when I turned six everything changed… Vincent started to act differently…He started to lock me in a room… and if I disobeyed him… he would beat me… then sexually abuse me," she said, starting to cry.

Theo wiped the tears away, comforting her, as he ran his fingers through her long strawberry blonde hair. He stayed quiet, hugging her while waiting for her to continue when she was ready.

"Then his friends… Malcom, Ivan, and Bruce …started to do the same… but they were a little more gentle… but I still hated it and them…They only fed me a small loaf of bread… and a small glass of water…every other day… I thought since I was bought by you… they would give up… What is going to…happen to me… when you can't be around me?" She asked, looking at his eyes with tears streaming down from hers.

"Nothing, because God will make sure they get exactly what they deserve. Let's finish our lunch, then I am taking you home, I will just keep the store closed the rest of the day. You don't need to try and work while you are in this state," he said, holding a nacho to her mouth. She took a bite and nodded.

They finished eating, then Theo took care of all of the animals. When he was finished, he grabbed her hand, and guided her out of the store. He locked the store's door and guided her to his car. He opened the door and helped her in.

He got in after and started to drive. He noticed a black car behind him so he went to town instead. He stopped at the mall and turned to Ela who looked confused. He began to speak.

"There is someone following us, so to protect you we are going to go into the mall to get you a phone to where if I am not around you, you can call me. Maybe we can lose them in the mall as well," he said. When he saw she nodded, he got out and went to her side.

He opened the door and helped her out. They went into the mall. He noticed Malcom, in a black hood following at a distance filming them. Theo took his jacket off again and put it over her head.

"They are filming us." Theo said, as Ela looked up at him confused. He put his arm around her shoulder and guided her faster into the mall. They went to the phone store and started to look around. Theo kept an eye on Malcom.

Ela chose a Samsung Galaxy S24 and they went to the counter to pay for it. She got a free case to go with it. They exited the store and went into the crowd, once they got to the crowd they went through a back exit to his car.

They got in the car, and Theo sped away. Theo stayed on the road to make sure they weren't being followed. Once the coast was clear, he drove home. They arrived home and put the car in the garage.

They went inside, and Theo locked the door behind him. He watched Ela go to her room to rest. He then went to the study. Before he could go in, Edna came into view with a shocked face.

"What's going on? Why are you both home so early?" She asked, coming close to him.

"Some people from Ela's past showed up at her store today. Trying to convince her to go back with him. They also taped horrible posters slandering her to her building" he said, as they walked into the study. Theo sat his stuff down, he sat at his desk as she sat across from him.

"Oh, goodness, is she okay?" She asked, with a worried expression.

"She was shaken up. I managed to calm her down. She is resting now. I will check on her in about an hour. First I have to do some background checks and send some evidence to the cops. Do you still have those pictures of the scars and bruises you took on her skin?" he said, pulling up his computer.

"Yeah, I sent them to you by email the first day she came," she said, standing up.

"Thank you, Do you want to light those soothing candles you have to help her relax, when she wakes up?" He asked, while typing.

"Yeah, I will," she said, leaving the study.

"Thank you," he said, while making a phone call.

He told the cops what was happening and sent them all the evidence. He then got up and walked up the stairs to check on Ela. He knocked on the door and listened but there was no answer.

He opened the door and looked inside, he saw she was sleeping, so he went back and closed her door. He went into the kitchen and started to make tea. Then he went back to the study to get some work done. He finished, just as he saw Ela come into the study.

"Hey, how are you feeling?" He asked, as he stood up.

"Better, but… I am… hungry," she said.

"Well then, let's make some food," he said, guiding her to the kitchen. She sat on a bar stool at the kitchen island and watched him cook. He was very aware of her eyes on him. He smiled to himself and continued to make spaghetti.

He finished the food and put it on plates. He placed a plate in front of her. They said the blessing and began to eat the food. They talked and laughed as they ate. Theo felt the connection between the two of them grow. He just wasn't sure she felt the same way.

He watched her as she finished her food. He blushed thinking about what the future would be like if he married her. The only problem was would she still stay with him, if she knew who he really was. He couldn't tell her the truth, not yet anyway.

He picked up their empty plates and took it to the sink and rinsed them off, then put them in the dishwasher. He smiled at her, noticing she was watching him. He led her to the living room.

He let her pick a movie she wanted to watch and they watched it till about eight thirty that night. They then did their Bible study and prayed with each other. She yawned and told him goodnight and went upstairs. He watched and made sure she went into her room. He took out his phone, and made a call.

"It's me. Get the job done. Get as much information you can out of them before handing them over to the cops. They will pay for what they have done," Theo said, giving a mischievous smirk and hanging up the phone. He then went to bed.

9

Feelings Emerge

I woke up at six o' clock. I got ready for church and went down stairs. I saw Theo at the bottom of the stairs and blushed as we made eye contact. What was happening to me? Why is it that whenever I see or get around him, it feels like there is a spark inside me.

'God, please help, I don't know what this feeling is. I want to completely trust him, but it feels like he is hiding something from me lately. Give me strength, Abba, in your holy name I pray amen.' I prayed as I made my way down the stairs to Theo.

"Hey, are you ready to go?" Theo asked me, as I stood beside him.

"Yes" I said, He put his hand on my back, and guided me out the door.

We got in his Mustang and headed to church with our Bibles in my lap. I looked over at him and he had a tense look on his face. He was wearing a navy blue tux, in which he looked really handsome.

I blushed as I looked down at the pink modest dress I was wearing. After a fifteen minute drive, we arrived at the church. Theo parked and cut the engine off and got out, he came to my side and opened the door and helped me out.

I handed him his Bible and he took it. He then took my hand and we headed into the church, all the ones who were there greeted us as we walked in. We worshiped God with the songs, then the preacher started the sermon.

The sermon was really good, it was about lying and how it not only affects us, but those around us. We walked out of church, I looked at Theo, and he looked uncomfortable. We got in the car and he started the engine.

"Hey, Theo… are you okay?" I asked, looking at him. He was startled from his thoughts and looked at me.

"Yeah, I am fine. Don't worry about it," he said, smiling, then drove out of the church parking lot.

We drove to the fancy restaurant and went inside. Theo was still lost in thought, and I kept wondering if he was hiding something from me. We were seated at the VIP table and handed menus.

We ordered steaks with different sides. The food only took fifteen minutes and it was brought to us. We blessed the food and started to eat. We didn't say a word to each other while we ate. I felt kind of sad as I watched him eat, while taking a bite of sweet potato fries.

Then all of a sudden, his phone rang. He had a shocked look on his face, then asked for me to stay here as he excused himself from the table. I watched him as he went outside to take the call. I kept thinking if he was really hiding something from me.

My heart started to feel hurt, I stopped eating and looked down at my hands in my lap. My thoughts started to run all over the place, I kept thinking if he was going to make me leave or even sell me, like Vincent did.

I shut my eyes tight so as to not cry, but the tears started to flow. I covered my face with my hands as the tears kept flowing down my face. I heard footsteps coming to the VIP section, I got my napkin and wiped them from my face. Theo came back into the area and sat down.

"Sorry, I had to take that call," Theo said, picking up his utensils again. He then looked at me because I didn't respond, and had a shocked look on his face. He got up and bent down to my side.

"Hey, what's wrong? What happened?" He asked me, taking my hand in his and using his other hand to guide my face to his to look at him. I just shook my head, I was afraid I would start crying again.

"Ela, please, tell me what is wrong, What happened while I was gone?" He asked, looking worried. I took a deep breath then asked, as tears started to flow again.

"Are… you … Going to… Sell me… and get rid… of me?" Tears were flowing harder when I got the last word out, I closed my eyes. Then all of a sudden I felt him gently pull me into a hug.

I opened my eyes wide, even though I couldn't see with all the tears. He then broke the hug and started to run his hand through my hair. He looked at me with a soft look, then put his forehead on mine.

"I am not going to sell you or get rid of you. You mean too much to me for that. I would never do anything to hurt you. I care about you, a lot," he said, closing his eyes. He then backed his head up and used his thumb to get rid of the tears on my face.

He then pulled his chair closer to me, and pulled my head against his chest again. His heart was beating rapidly. He kept me there till I calmed down. When he saw I had calmed down to where I wasn't crying so much, he started to talk again.

"Why would you think I would sell you or get rid of you?" He asked, using his thumb and first finger to lift my chin so my eyes would meet his.

"You… have… been… distant… and …it …looked …like you… weren't happy." I said, as I stared into his eyes. He smiled at me and hugged me again, as he wiped the rest of my tears away.

"I have just been dealing with some troublesome things, I am really happy that you are by my side, that I even met you. I want to protect you, help you to learn more experiences and even to guide you in your walk with God. Ela, I love you," he said, giving a gentle smile.

"I… I don't know… how to… love," I said, looking down. He lifted my chin again and looked in my eyes.

"Do you feel your heart race? Do you feel a kind of giddy feeling when you are around me? Do you feel like you would want to do anything for me?" he said, and I nodded. "Then that is love. You care about me a lot, to the point that when I distanced myself, it made you sad, and for that I am sorry. Ela, if you can forgive me, will you be my girlfriend?"

"Yes," I said. I then took the initiative and kissed his cheek. We both blushed, then he started to feed me while smiling. We finished our food, paid and left. He held my hand as we drove back to the house. Edna had gone to lunch with her friends after church.

We arrived at the house and went in. Then I started to hear music behind me. I turned around and Theo grabbed me and pulled me close.

"Let's dance," he said, as he took my hand and we started to dance together. I couldn't dance so I kept stepping on his toes. Theo said they had moved the date of the company party to next weekend, to give people more time.

We danced to the music and laughed and talked. Then it was time to go back to church. We went back to church. We listened to the sermon. Then we went back home. We all got ready for bed. We went to bed after watching a TV show.

10

She Can't Know about This

Theo woke up and got ready in a suit, then packed some leather clothes in a bag. He went and put the bag in the trunk of the Bugatti. He came back in and saw Ela coming down stairs. He met her at the bottom of the stairs and pulled her close to him and gave her a hug.

"I will be late coming home today, so Assistant Scott will take you home at the end of the day." Theo said, as he led Ela to the car, while giving her a bag that had her breakfast and lunch.

"Okay" She told him. He kissed her forehead and helped her into the car. Theo drove to her work place, and hugged her bye. He then went to his company and started to work until eleven thirty.

He went to his Assistant's desk and started to talk to him. Telling him not to forget about Ela and that he wouldn't be back at the office today. He went down to his car and got his bag out. He changed his clothes and started to drive. He arrived at a building, he put a mask on and went inside.

He walked for a while and went into the soundproof basement. He met two other men, and started to discuss a plan. The two men started to give all the information they had.

"Have they confessed to what they have done yet? We can't hand them to the police until they confess." Theo said to the two men.

"One of them has confessed to locking the girl up, but the rest of them aren't talking." the two men said, unlocking the door.

"Good, let's keep trying to get more information out of them." Theo said, walking into the room. He stared at the four men tied to chairs. He got a bucket and splashed them with water. They woke up with a jerk.

"Are you all going to talk, or do we have to keep trying to get it out of you?" Theo said, crossing his arms.

"YOU ARE A CRAZY PSYCHO, WHO ARE YOU?!" Vincent screamed, trying to get loose.

"You don't need to know who I am, you just need to know that I can get anything I want from you so easily. It just takes a little bit of convincing." Theo said, pulling out a knife.

"Tell me did you have fun, kidnapping an orphan girl and sexually assaulting her repeatedly then beating her?" Theo said walking circles around Vincent. He glared at the others who just looked down at the floor in silence. Theo then walked to the others and put the knife close to them where they could see it. He stared into their eyes.

"Do any of you have anything to say? We already know what you did, I just want to hear you say it. So say it, you had no fears, right?" Theo said, Giving them a stern look.

"Fine, don't talk, men, douse them with freezing water and starve them till they fess up." Theo said, turning to his men. As soon as Theo was about to leave Malcom fessed up.

"Okay, okay, WE DID IT, WE LOCKED HER IN A ROOM AND WOULD TAKE TURNS SEXUALLY ASSAULTING HER, BUT Vincent WAS THE ONLY ONE WHO BEAT HER!!" Malcom said.

"Perfect, now we can hand you over to the police, men make sure they get their justice," Theo said, walking out.

He walked out of the building and got in his car, he changed clothes and headed home. He stopped by a small flower shop that was about to close up and got Ela some flowers. He then went home and walked in the door.

The house was quiet, but the TV was still on, but on low volume. He walked into the living room and saw Ela asleep on the couch. He chuckled to himself and bent down beside her. He moved her hair out of her face and kissed her cheek.

"Ela, wake up, princess," Theo said, shaking her shoulder. "Ela... princess, wake up,"

"Mmmm… you're home?" Ela said, waking up.

"Yeah, I am home, I am sorry I am so late. But I got you something" Theo said, helping her to sit up.

"You got… me flowers," Ela said, taking the flowers and smelling them.

"Yeah, I am not sure if you have a favorite so I got you one of every flower the shop had. Do you forgive me for being late?" Theo said.

"Mhm" Ela said, nodding. She hugged him which caught Theo off guard. Then he hugged her back.

"If you are sleepy, you don't have to wait for me. You could have gone to bed." Theo said, pushing her hair behind her ears.

"I… wanted to," Ela said.

"Okay, princess, but it is time to go to bed," he said. He took the flowers from her and instructed the new maid to put them in a vase. He picked Ela up princess style and took her up the stairs. He let her down at her bedroom door.

"Go get you some sleep now, I will see you in the morning, princess," Theo said. He kissed her on the forehead. He watched her go in and he shut the door. He then headed to his room and got ready for bed.

He was gonna turn those idiots in tomorrow with the cops. He laid in bed and dreamed about his future with Ela. Then all of sudden, his dream turned into a nightmare. Where Ela had found out he was an undercover spy and left him.

He woke up suddenly, sweating, he got out of bed and went to Ela's room. He slightly opened the door and looked in. He saw Ela peacefully sleeping. He sighed and closed the door. He went down stairs and got a glass of water.

He drank a glass of water, then went back upstairs. When he passed by Ela's room, he heard her screaming. He panicked and burst into her room. When he got in there, she was gone. He searched around.

"ELA, PRINCESS WHERE ARE YOU?!" he said.

He got out his phone and started to make calls. He then got dressed in the leather suit and mask and ran down stairs and outside.

He got in his black Mustang and headed out. He kept thinking to himself. *How did anyone get in and take her? The bedrooms are on the second floor.*

He met his men at an alley and informed the police. They racked their brains on who would take her. Then Theo realized he has an enemy who is the most feared mafia. That dude has been trying to kill him for years. They headed out to all the known spots the mafia person has. There was nothing though, so they kept looking all night and morning.

11

Scared and Kidnapped

I woke up, tied to a chair. My mouth was taped shut, I couldn't move or speak. My body started to tremble again. My mind kept going back to Theo. Will I be able to see him again? Am I going to be able to hear his encouraging voice again? Am I going to die?

I started to tear up, but tried to hold the tears back. I heard someone coming and looked up. A man in all black and a mask, with white hair came into the room. I tried to struggle out of the ropes.

"Hello, darling… don't worry, I am not going to hurt you. I just kidnapped you to make your boyfriend pay for all he has done. Once he finds where you are we will have a trap set for him and he will die," he said, then left the room.

My body trembled even more, Why does he want to kill Theo? Why use me? What is going to happen to Theo? I started to cry, I prayed to God '*Please help Theo, Help him to make it out alive. Please help him to have enough strength to do what he needs to do in order to survive*'

I cried myself to sleep. I woke up to the sound of screaming. I looked around but couldn't see anyone. I tried to struggle out of the ropes again, but it didn't work. I heard footsteps coming so I pretended to be asleep.

"Wake up darling, Your boyfriend is taking forever to show up so we are going to show him just what we are capable of. We will send him a video of us lightly tormenting you. That will get him to show up. Douse her with water boys," he said.

They poured freezing cold water on me. My body trembled even more now. Then he lit a cigarette and started to place the burning part on my skin. I screamed out in pain, but they were muffled. The tears started to flow again, as I watched him. One of his men then pulled my hair and put a knife to my neck, all while the white haired dude was videoing me.

"If you want your precious girlfriend back, then come find her. I will say, it won't be easy on you. If you don't come and find her within three days, I will use her as I please and might even kill her. You better hurry Theodore" he said, cutting the video off afterwards.

He and his men then left the room. The burns ached and my body trembled. I began to cry again. This time I couldn't fall asleep so easily. The pain was unbearable, I had forgotten all of the pain I had felt from Vincent.

Then all those memories started to come back into my mind. I started to panic and cry harder. My body is trembling more and more. I could feel I was going back to the emotionless phase again.

I don't remember going to sleep, but when I woke up my body was in pain from the burns. I looked up feeling no emotions and saw the white haired dude come in. He looked at me smiling.

"Well, soon your boyfriend will be here and you will get to watch him die," he said, laughing to himself. I just stared at him, I didn't feel like showing any emotions, I just felt numb.

All of a sudden we started to hear gunshots in the distance. People started to scream and what sounded like a lot of people running. Then the door burst open and five mystery men in all black came in.

The white haired dude looked shocked. He tried to reach for his gun but was shot with a tranquilizer by one of the men. Another man came rushing towards me. He looked at me with worry in his eyes. Who was he? Why was he worried?

"Princess, thank God you are okay. Did he hurt you at all?" The mystery man asked, I just stared at him.

"Princess? It's me, Theo" he said, pulling down his mask, revealing his face. I just stared blankly at him.

He untied me from the chair and picked me up like he always does and brought me out. I didn't feel like doing anything. He brought me to the doctor and they examined me, they said I had emotional numbing, and that the burns will heal with medicine.

They explained to him that my emotions could come back within time, and that I lost them because of a traumatic event. He then thanked the doctor and looked at me, he sat beside me on the bed and looked at me.

"I promise, I will help you to get your emotions back. We will get you talking again. I won't let anything else bad happen to you. First though, I am gonna have to finally tell you the truth about me," he said, while we waited for the discharge papers.

"I am an undercover spy and I manage a small gang, but I don't kill people. I work with the police to capture criminals and get them to confess, then I hand them to the police," he said, looking at my eyes. I nodded and he continued.

"I do have enemies though. They will use any means necessary to get to me and try to kill me, because I destroy their plans. I won't let them get you ever again. I am just blessed that you are safe with me again and Grandma was not in the house when it happened. I completely understand if you don't want to be around me anymore though," he said, with a sad expression on his face.

I scooted closer to him and put my head on his shoulder. I felt his body tense for a moment then relax again. He put his arm around my shoulders and we just sat there in silence.

"Does this mean you are going to stay by my side?" He asked. I nodded.

Even though I couldn't feel anything, I knew God had a plan for us both. The nurse came back in with a clipboard and papers. Theo grabbed the papers and handed them to me, helping me when I needed it.

He then picked me up again princess style and carried me back to his car. We rode back home and went inside. Edna was there at the door waiting for us. She came to me and hugged me tight.

"Oh dear, I heard what happened. I am so sorry dear. We will do everything in our power to keep you safe and help you to get back to the person you were becoming," she said, letting go of the hug and holding my hands. I nodded and went upstairs.

I heard Edna and Theo talking about me and different plans they can do to help me get my emotions back. I went into my room and got ready for bed. I put the medicine on the burns and layed down.

12

Helping Her

Theo stayed up all night in the study, trying to figure out how to help Ela get her emotions back and get her to talk again. He looked on Google and researched a bunch of different things.

"A person with emotional numbness needs regular activity, a healthy and balanced diet, support from loved ones, and working with a mental health professional."

Theo called his assistant and told him to find the best mental health professional in the country, price does not matter. He then went to the kitchen and started to prepare a healthy and balanced diet for her.

He went upstairs and into Ela's room. He crouched beside her bed and moved the hair out of her face. He touched her face and kissed her forehead.

"Ela, princess, wake up. You can't sleep all day, I have got a plan to help you. Come on, princess," he said.

She woke up and put her arms around his neck. She still didn't talk or show any emotions on her face. Theo picked her up princess style (or bridal style) and took her downstairs.

He placed her at the table beside Edna. He sat across from her after talking to the maid about the diet for her. He sat down, and they blessed the food. He watched her as she took small bites of her food. Once they finished, Ela just sat there.

"Go upstairs and get dressed, I am gonna take you on a walk through the park. It is time you be surrounded by God's creations" Theo said, taking her hand and guiding her to the stairs.

Ela nodded and headed upstairs. He went upstairs and took a shower and got ready for the day. He then made a phone call to his cop friends, Avery and Liam, letting them know about the situation and the plan.

He knew Avery and Liam would gladly help out. He met them a few years ago when they were investigating a case about a dangerous mafia boss, named Jace. He went to their wedding, and now they are expecting a baby girl in five months.

They made plans to meet at the park. Ela came down the stairs in jeans and a T-shirt. She stopped beside him. He pulled her close and kissed her forehead and guided her to the door, and put her shoes on for her.

"Princess, are you ready to go? I got some friends that are going to meet us at the park." Theo asked.

Ela nodded, and they walked out of the door. They got in the Bugatti and rode thirty minutes to the park. Theo helped her out of the car and held her hand. They started to walk to the entrance.

"Ela, this is Avery and Liam, They are the cops I work with to take down criminals." Theo said, Ela nodded, as they said nice to meet you.

They all started to walk the park, talking and enjoying the scenery. Theo kept hold of Ela's hand and occasionally kissed her forehead, when she looked like she was getting uncomfortable. He reassured her every time.

They stopped at a picnic area and rested for Avery. Theo was standing talking to Liam, when he noticed Ela looking at flowers and smelling them. She then looked at him and gave a slight smile.

His face went into shock, then smiled. Liam started to poke fun at him. Theo sent up a prayer to God asking him to help get Ela's emotions back and her voice back. They then joined the women where they were sitting.

"Princess, I love you" Theo whispered in Ela's ear. Ela's eyes went wide as she looked at him with a small blush on her face. He then grabbed her and kissed her forehead, as Avery and Liam smiled. Liam went to a little food cart and brought back cotton candy for the women. Then Theo heard a whisper from Ela, which he barely missed.

"*Thank you*" She looked up at Theo and stood on her tiptoes and whispered in his ear. "*I love you*"

Theo was shocked, then smiled and hugged her again. He held her shoulders, as she ate her cotton candy. They stayed and talked for a while till Avery got tired, then Avery and Liam went home.

Theo then guided Ela to the car and headed to the fancy restaurant, where he and Ela started their relationship. He helped her out of the car and went inside the restaurant. They got their usual seats. They ordered their food and Theo pulled out a jewelry box and pushed it across the table toward Ela. She looked from the box to him multiple times. Then she stared at him.

"Open it, It is for you, my princess" Theo said, watching her.

She opened the box and then started crying, with a smile. Theo's plan worked, she was starting to get her emotions back. He moved his chair closer to her and put the necklace on her. He then pulled her head towards his shoulder. He put his hands around her shoulders and ran his fingers through her hair.

"I love you so much, princess. I want to protect you with everything I have. I am sorry I never told you about who I was, and why I was so distant. I thought I could protect you that way, but again God had other plans." Theo said, kissing her forehead.

After he got her calmed down, the waitress brought the food to the table. He started to feed Her as she smiled at him. Then all of a sudden, she kissed him and he kissed back.

"I love you… Theo" Ela said, smiling at him. He smiled back at her and kissed her forehead again.

"I love you too, princess." Theo said.

They finished their food and paid, leaving the restaurant. He helped Ela into the car then took her to a public fountain. He then made a phone call and hung up. He told Ela to look in the sky.

Fireworks started to go off, as he held Ela by his side, watching her, while she watched the fireworks. Her face lit up in amusement, as she watched them. He thanked God several times for giving her back her emotions.

He was so happy. When the fireworks stopped he turned her face, with his thumb and index finger, to his and kissed her. It felt like the whole world paused as they shared this moment with God. Then they went home, had supper, and got ready for bed.

13

Gaining Everything Back along with Confidence

I woke up the next morning, actually feeling happy. I fiddled with the necklace Theo gave me as my heart raced as I thought about him. I got ready for the day by doing the morning routine and putting on a modest dress. I then went downstairs and saw Edna at the table. I sat down, as the maid put a plate in front me.

"Thank you" I said to the maid then turned to Edna. "Where is Theo?"

"Oh, dear, he had to go in early, he had to take care of some things. I am glad you are back to yourself." Edna said, putting her hand on mine.

"Me too," I said. Then I took a bite of food. I finished my food then went to the living room. I prayed and talked to God, thanking him for everything and to keep Theo safe. I then turned to the book of Proverbs and read the whole book.

Then I heard the phone Theo got for me go off. I got it and looked at the phone. I unlocked the screen and saw that Theo had texted me. I opened the message and read.

'Hey, princess, I am sorry I couldn't be there when you woke up. I promise I will see you when I get home, I will get off early. I love you. You can spend the day with Grandma'

I texted back. *'It is okay. I love you too. Okay'.* Then I went to see what Edna was doing. She told me she was gonna go shopping with some friends and told me I could join. I agreed and we went outside when her friends arrived.

We went to the mall and started to walk around. We bought different things such as dresses and other clothes, accessories, soaps and other things. We then went to eat at a little cafe.

Once we were done eating, Edna suggested we go to Theo's company to give him a surprise, so her friends dropped us off at his company. We went in with our arms interlocked. Edna and I went to the front desk and she told them to lead us to Theo's office.

The lady didn't seem very happy to do it, but recognized Edna. She gave me an evil look, then showed us the elevator to take us to his office. We went in the elevator and pressed the button to his office.

We knew he was in a meeting, so we went onto the floor of his office. Assistant Scott greeted us and led us to the waiting area of his office. He gave us coffee and we talked for a while. We then got up and went to the personal library Theo had behind his desk.

We picked out the books we wanted to read and read them while we waited for him. He then came in and looked surprised that we were here. Edna hugged him and whispered something to him, then left.

I stood up and walked to his side. He grabbed my waist and pulled me close to him. I smiled, as he started to kiss my forehead. He guided me towards the waiting area again.

"I am so happy you are here. I am so exhausted. I missed you," he said, I giggled.

"I missed you too, but this was all Edna's idea." I said, as he held my hand.

We talked for a while and even laughed. Then he had to go to another meeting, so he asked Assistant Scott to send me and Edna home. I kissed him and hugged him then we all left his office.

We went home and put our stuff away. I put the gift I bought Theo on his study desk. I then went upstairs and to the balcony. I got my book and started to read. I was trying to learn more and more.

I borrowed a bunch of books from Theo's study. I read until I saw Theo's car come in the driveway. I put the book away and went downstairs to meet him. I waited at the door with a smile on my face. His face lit up when he saw me at the door, he came to me and hugged me and kissed my forehead.

"Hey princess. Did you have a good day?" Theo asked.

"Yes" I said, While hugging him back.

I hung on to his arm, as we went into the dining room. We sat at the table, as the maid brought our food to us. Edna said the blessing and we began to eat. We talked about each other's day.

When we finished, I watched as Theo excused himself from the table and went to his study. I excused myself and followed him at a distance. I stopped at the door and looked in. I noticed him pick up the gift and open it. He smiled and took the watch out of the box.

"Ela, princess, I know you are there. Come here." Theo said, looking at the door.

I went inside the study, as he looked at me. I watched him as he put the watch on with a proud look on his face. I smiled and stood at the entrance. He grabbed my waist and pulled me close, he hugged me as I hugged him back.

"Thank you for the watch. I love it, but I told you to use the card on yourself, not me." Theo said, still holding me close.

"I did, but you got me this necklace and you are always providing me with stuff, I wanted to get you something." I said. I started learning how to speak normally and now I don't have to pause to try to speak.

"I love you princess," he said, kissing my forehead.

"I love you too," I said, leaning my head on his shoulder.

We stayed in the hug for a while, before we stepped apart and he sat at his desk and started to type away at his computer. I smiled at him then exited the study. I didn't want to disturb him when he was trying to work.

I went back upstairs and back to the balcony and started to read my book again. The week went by pretty fast and the party was tomorrow. So I was trying to learn as much as I can about etiquette and manners.

The sun was starting to set, I put my book on the table of the balcony, stood up and watched the sunset. I talked to God while I watched it. It was nice to be truly loved and be free. The small garden we had was being illuminated by the sunset.

It was all beautiful and I thanked God so much. Everything felt perfect, almost like a fairy tale. I heard Theo come out but I didn't turn around. He came up behind me and wrapped his arms around my waist. His face was near my ear.

"What are you doing princess?" He whispered in my ear.

"Watching God's creation," I said, smiling.

"That is great," he said, still holding me in his arms.

I leaned back on his shoulder and we watched the sunset together. We were just enjoying each other's company and God's presence. Everything felt like a dream. I thanked God once again for everything.

14

The Party

Theo woke up the next morning and got ready for work. He knew the party was this afternoon, he couldn't wait to dance with Ela. He walked down stairs and saw Ela waiting for him, laughing with his grandmother.

He walked to her side, wrapped his arm around her waist, and gave her a kiss on the forehead. Edna gave an all knowing look. Ela smiled up at him. He kept hold of her waist.

"You are up early. Ready to go? Did you pack your dress for this afternoon?" He asked Ela.

"I did," she said with a nod.

"Grandma, I will send Assistant Scott to come get you this afternoon and bring you to the party" he said, as she nodded.

They walked out of the house and headed off to work. Once he dropped off Ela at her building, he went to his company. His assistant greeted him and told him the schedule for today. He got to work on signing the documents.

He then went to the meeting room to start the meeting, with the sales and market department. The meeting was long, with a lot of arguing and debating. Theo got them on the same page and told them to get to work.

He went back to his office and texted Ela. *"How is your lunch going? I wish I could have lunch with you, but I will see you this afternoon to get you for the party."* He put his phone away and started on his email and other things on his computer.

The work day was long and hard. Everything was finished though. He changed into his party tux and left. He went to Ela's building and saw her closing up with her beautiful dress on. He came up behind her and hugged her, while she was shocked.

They then made their way to the party. They entered, arms interlocked with each other. People started to stare and whisper. He noticed she got nervous, he pulled her closer to him, his hand on her waist, as they walked through the crowd.

They met Edna close to the food table. They all started to talk and laugh. Then an announcer said they were starting the dancing. He offered his hand to Ela.

"Care to dance, my lady?" He asked, looking like a gentleman.

She took his hand and he guided her to the dance floor. He put his other hand on her waist. They slowly danced to the music, and all eyes were on them. They stole the show with all the dancers.

Theo didn't notice his childhood best friend, looking mad. All of his attention was on Ela, as they danced and laughed. At the end of the song, they slowed their dancing, Theo pulled her closer and kissed her.

Everything around them felt like it stopped. Everyone was taking pictures and gasping. They stayed there kissing for a short time, then broke away and stared into each other's eyes. Then Theo's childhood friend picked up a glass of champagne and stormed over to them, throwing the champagne at Ela.

Theo blocked it just in time, as it hit the back of his tux. He let go of Ela and turned around, facing his best friend. June, his best friend, looked at his mad face. Everyone stopped moving, looking surprised.

"June, what is your problem?" He asked her, still protecting Ela.

"WHY ARE YOU PROTECTING HER, YOU BLEW ME OFF TO GO TO THIS WITH HER! YOU DON'T KNOW WHO SHE REALLY IS! SHE IS A -"

"ENOUGH! I KNOW EXACTLY WHO SHE IS. I LOVE HER, stop it now, this isn't the place or the time for this, you need to leave" Theo said, turning back to Ela and hugging her.

June started to cry as people recorded, and she ran out of the party. Theo guided Ela out to the balcony and told everyone to continue to have fun. They went to the balcony and Ela tried to help clean his tux.

"Princess, it's okay, as long as you are safe that is all that matters" he said, grabbing her hands gently.

"But-" she said, as he pulled her close and hugged her. The wind lightly blowing their hair.

"I am fine, I love you princess. No one will hurt you ever again." Theo said, hugging her.

They stayed there for a while, Edna watched them through the doorway. She smiled and went back. Then Theo guided Ela back inside.

They continued to talk and have fun, enjoying each other's company and the party. Everyone was complimenting her beauty and that they looked like a wonderful couple. Then the company auction began.

Theo and Ela watched as the auction went on. Edna told Theo to buy the diamond necklace they put up for auction and give to Ela. He looked at Ela and started bidding. He won the bid and went up to collect the necklace, while guiding Ela up there with him.

Theo received the necklace and went behind Ela. He put the necklace on her. She looked at him surprised, because he paid five hundred thousand dollars for it. He kissed her in front of everyone, again.

He guided her back down off the stage and stood next to Edna. The auction ended and music began to play again. They danced for a while, grabbing everyone's attention once more. They enjoyed the night.

At midnight, the party ended. Everyone went home, Theo kissed Ela good night as he watched her go up the stairs to her room. He went to his room and got ready for bed. He stared at the picture they took together at the party.

He smiled to himself, and laid down. He started to dream about the future, imagining marrying her and having a family with her. He didn't realize he fell asleep, waking up that Saturday morning. He sat up and stretched, yawning.

He got up and got dressed in casual clothes. He walked down stairs. He saw Ela and Edna at the table chatting and eating breakfast. He walked up to them smiling.

"Good morning," he said, planting a kiss on Ela's forehead.

He sat down across from her, as the maid brought his breakfast. He blessed his food and started to eat, watching Ela chat and laugh with his grandmother. He loved her laugh. His phone started to ring and he excused himself from the table.

He looked at the name on the screen, 'June'. He declined the call, but she called back immediately. He made an annoyed face and answered. Wishing he could block her number.

"Hello?" he said, annoyance in his voice.

"Theo, can we please meet and talk? I want to clear things up with you," she said,

"Fine," he said, with a sigh.

15

Feeling Special

I was chatting with Edna, when Theo came back into the room. He whispered in my ear to follow him, as he took my hand and guided me from the table. Edna smiled and continued to finish eating.

"Theo, what's wrong? What happened?" I asked, placing my hand on his cheek. He leaned into my touch.

"June called, wanting me to meet her. I want you to go with me, so she can properly apologize to you." Theo said. "Go get ready. We are going to meet her at a cafe in an hour."

"Okay" I said, placing a kiss on his cheek, then going to my room.

I changed into a floral print dress and put some heels on. I put on a little makeup and the necklace Theo gave me yesterday. I looked over myself in the mirror, feeling like I have truly become someone who is confident, not only in myself but with my walk with God as well.

I walked downstairs, as Theo stared at me. I blushed hard, feeling his eyes on me as I came down the stairs. He held his hand out and I took it. He twirled me and pulled me in close for a kiss.

"Are you ready, princess?" Theo asked.

"Yes," I said, confidently. Feeling positive and confident.

We walked to his lamborghini and got in. We drove to the cafe, and he helped me out. Holding my waist as we walked in. June saw us walk in together and her face shifted. Then she put on a fake smile and stood up. We walked over to her.

"Theo, sit" She motioned to a chair beside her.

He pulled out the two chairs across from her. We both sat down. The tension and the awkwardness hung in the air. It was silent for a long while. Then Theo spoke up.

"What did you want to talk about?" he said, holding my hand on the table where she could see.

"I wanted to say, I am sorry for my actions at the party. I was jealous," she said, watching our hands. I tried to move my hand away, but he held it firm.

"It's not me you should be apologizing to, but her." Theo said, looking at me.

"I'm sorry," she said, looking at me, with a sigh. It was obvious she was still jealous.

"It's fine," I said, awkward to be put in this situation.

She then excused herself, with a fake smile, and left the cafe. Theo picked up my hand and kissed it. I blushed and looked down. He chuckled as we both stood up and walked out. He guided me to the park that was beside the cafe.

We walked the park hand in hand. He stood out a lot as people stared at us. He smiled at me and put his hand around my waist. We stopped by a fountain and sat on the edge. We talked and laughed.

A lot of people watched us, but we weren't phased by it. Being around him always made me feel special. I felt like I was his only one. I felt like a princess. We found an ice cream cart and got some.

We ate our ice cream, laughing and having fun. We spent all day together, just having a date. What we didn't know was that June had hired a person to spy on us and get incriminating evidence on us.

We finished off the day by doing a Bible study in the garden. We read the book of James. It was nice to have someone, who I could learn more about God with. Once the sun went down, we went back inside. We got ready for bed, and went to sleep.

I woke up the next morning, got ready for church. I put on a modest red dress and some black heels. I put on the necklace with some other jewelry. I curled my hair, and put on a little makeup.

I grabbed my Bible and headed downstairs, after putting on some perfume. I saw Theo talking to Edna in the living room. He looked up at me and blushed. I blushed as well as I made it to the bottom of the stairs.

We went to church and listened to the sermon titled "God's Purpose for Our Lives." Everyone at church was so nice, always including me and hugging me. We left church at twelve and went to eat at the Mexican restaurant.

We ordered our food and talked for a while. Edna brings up stories of Theo's childhood, which made him blush. This moment felt like I was actually a part of a family. Feeling loved and treasured.

The food arrived and we blessed our food. We began to eat and talk. Theo got a phone call and excused himself from the table. Edna and I kept talking, Theo came back, with an angry and worried look on his face.

"We have to get out of here. Somebody released pictures of us yesterday, with a made up story of how we were faking our relationship. If we don't hurry, the paparazzi will start showing up soon," he said, taking my hand.

I grabbed my purse, while Edna did the same. We started to walk out of the restaurant when vans pulled up. Cameras started to flash, as microphones were shoved in our faces.

Theo blocked my face with his arm, holding me tight against him. Reporters started to ask questions really fast. They crowded around us. Theo stood tall and put his hand up.

"ENOUGH!" he said, as they quieted down. "We will answer all questions at a press conference, in a few days. But right now, this is not the time or place for this. If you were actually good reporters, you would figure out something isn't right about these rumors, now if you will excuse us we have somewhere to be" Theo said, in an over-powering type of way.

We made our way through the crowd of shocked reporters. Theo kept my face hidden as we walked. We all made it to his car and got in. Edna climbed in the back seat. Theo drove away as the reporters tried to follow.

We made it back home. We went inside and Theo went to his study. I followed him, he grabbed my waist and pulled me close to him, while he talked to his assistant over the phone to schedule a press conference. He then hung up and put his head on my shoulder.

"I am sorry, you got caught up in this mess," he said, sighing.

"It's okay. Who do you think spread the rumor" I said, I had a guess but didn't want to say anything with no proof.

"I don't know but we will get to the bottom of it," he said. We stayed hugging for a while.

Theo locked all doors as reporters started to show up out of nowhere. I watched as he continued to talk on the phone. He kept making call after call. He looked exhausted, so I made him some pastries and some coffee. I took the things to his study and placed them on his desk.

He looked at me and smiled, holding my hand as he continued to talk on the phone. I could tell he was stressed. He finally hung up and sighed.

I felt bad for him. He had to handle so much, but no matter how many times I ask him if I could help, he just tells me to just wait and show up with him at the press conference. I massaged his head, while he ate the pastries.

I could help this way, by keeping him less stressed. I didn't like seeing him like this, but I know this is what he has to do. Night came, and he told me to go to bed. I kissed his cheek and agreed even though I didn't want to.

I reluctantly went to bed. I kept tossing and turning, worrying about Theo. So I sat up, and prayed to God. *Heavenly father, we need you. We need your guidance. I pray for Theo. help him through this tough time. Give him strength and comfort. Give him rest. Give us all the right words to say at the press conference. Lord, let your will be done and let the rumors disappear. In Your holy name I pray. Amen*

I went downstairs, and went into his study. I looked inside. He was working hard, but the dark circles under his eyes were evident. What can I do to help him? I remembered I had social media on my phone, but would going on social media really help?

I texted his Assistant, *"would it help if I go live on social media and explain my story to them?"* I waited for his response. He texted back *"It might help, but if it gets too overwhelming, shut it down"*

I texted back okay and started to set up everything. I prayed to God to give me the right words to say. "Hi, my name is Ela. A lot of you know me by now, by the rumors going around about me and Theo. First I want to clarify, we are not faking our relationship one bit. I love him and I am sure he loves me. Those pictures that are showing me with no clothes, I will explain. Yes, I am not a virgin anymore, but it wasn't by choice. Ever since I could remember, I was an orphan, I don't know my parents or even my last name. The person who took those photos was a person I lived with, and the only person I knew. When I got older, he became different. He would beat me and sexually assault me so much that I stopped speaking. I lost all emotions because of him. Those pictures were what he called his 'trophies'. He would take those after he did what he pleased. Then one day he sold me to some people who then sold me at an auction. That is how I met Theo. He bought me at that auction and took me home. He healed my wounds and helped me to feel safe. He helped me find my voice and emotions. He made me feel safe. He showed me God's love and helped me to get saved and grow with God. Our feelings started to grow for each other as we spent more time with each other. I hope this helps to clarify anything. We will answer questions at the press conference in about two days. Thanks for listening to my story."

I cut the live off and sighed, hopefully that helped Theo. I stood up and was about to clean up, when I felt arms wrap around my waist. I looked over my shoulder at Theo. I smiled at him and put my hand on his head.

"You were incredible and so brave. I am so proud of you. You didn't have to put yourself out there for me though," he said.

"I wanted to help, so I texted your assistant to see if this would, he said it should, so hopefully it did" I said.

He twirled me around in his arms and kissed my forehead. Then pulled away smiling, hugging me for some time. I was glad, it seems he was more at ease than he was before. We hugged for a while, then Edna came into the living room.

"Theo, there are more reporters outside. They don't seem like they want to wait for the press conference." Edna said.

"It's fine, I will get the guards to get them to leave. They can't come in anyway without the code and the windows aren't breakable" Theo said, holding my waist.

We watched the night service of church through social media, as we can't get out of the house at the moment. It was good. We finished and saw the guards forcing people to leave. Theo instructed the maid to fix something to eat.

We went into the dining room and ate the best smelling chicken with rice and vegetables. We talked about how the press conference would go down. We talked about Theo's plan for the press conference.

We finished and got ready for bed. I prayed to God to help us at the press conference, and that everything would go well. I also prayed for Theo. I dozed off to sleep, peacefully.

16

The Press Conference

Theo woke up the morning of the press conference and got ready. He said a quick prayer and headed downstairs. He saw Ela at the bottom of the stairs, looking nervous.

"It is going to be okay, God knows what he is doing, God has got us." Theo said.

Theo grabbed Ela by her waist and gave her a quick kiss, before guiding her and his grandmother to the vehicle. The guards kept reporters at a distance. They drove to the press conference.

They arrived and headed inside. They went on the stage and the press conference began.

"Mr. Ambrose, is your relationship just a contract between you and Ela?" one reporter said.

"No, it is not a contract relationship. We love each other and are dating each other in a normal way" Theo said, into the microphone.

"Ela, did you want attention by doing that live, the other day?" another reporter asked.

"No, I did that live to tell my story and the truth" I said, as Theo looked mad. I held his hand.

"Mr. Ambrose, so are the rumors false? Are you saying someone is framing you two?" Another reporter asked, as the lights flash from the cameras

"The rumors are not true. Someone is framing us and I have the evidence, these past few days I have been gathering evidence. As my assistant shows. The rumor comes from an anonymous IP address.

We traced the IP address and found out it was June Setler, the fashion designer." Theo said, as a picture of her comes on the screen behind us.

Everyone gasped as multiple pictures were taken. Reporters started to talk among each other. We watched the screen as a video showed June paying a mysterious person and handing that person a yellow envelope.

"Mr. Ambrose, can you explain why the top designer would do that?" a reporter asked.

"Simple, She is jealous of Ela. She has feelings for me and I never reciprocated her feelings. When I started dating Ela, it made her mad with jealousy. You already saw how she tried to throw champagne at Ela. Why not believe she would do this?" Theo said, with a stern look.

Theo stood and grabbed Ela's hand. They all walked off the stage as Theo's assistant took over, saying that was the end of the press conference and thank you for attending. They walked out and sat in the car.

They watched as all the reporters started to run to their cars and sped off. Ela watched them confused. Where were they going so fast? Ela looked at Theo, who smiled at her.

"They are going to June's place to get information on why she did it. They are all about getting stories, especially on well known people." Theo said, holding her hand.

They drove to a cafe. They ate lunch and talked. Then Theo paid and drove them to the mall. He told Ela and Edna to buy whatever they wanted. They walked from store to store.

Theo got stuck with carrying all of the bags, while Edna interlocked her arms with Ela's. Theo watched Ela smile and laugh, his heart filling with joy. He talked to God, thanking him for everything.

They were on the news that afternoon. Theo watched as they showed the press conference on the news. Everything they said, and the actions that took place. Then the news showed reporters confronting June and asking her different questions.

She looked like she was playing the victim. Then she tried to run away from the reporters several times. Essentially locking herself up in her house. Theo watched the screen, then made a phone call.

"Scott, release all the evidence we have on June. She can't play the victim, when she is not one. Thanks" Theo said, hanging up the phone.

Theo walked to the window that reached from the roof to the floor. He watched Ela and Edna talking and hanging out in the garden. He talked to God to help him to get the truth revealed.

He smiled at Ela, then went into his study. He started making emails and researching stuff. He saved all the info he had on June and sent it to his Assistant. He gave the information to Liam, his cop friend.

He printed all the stuff off and put them in a folder, and hid the folder in a secret spot in the study. Theo and his assistant worked a while till Ela came into the study. He noticed she brought some refreshments.

"Hey, princess," Theo said, grabbing and holding her hand.

"Hey, you know you don't have to do this to June, I am used to being blamed for stuff," Ela said, holding his hand.

"Princess, I told you ever since you met me, I would take care of and protect you. I won't let anyone harm you. June has been spoiled and now she has to pay the consequences of her actions," Theo said, standing up hugging her and placing a kiss on her forehead.

They stayed in the hug for some time, enjoying being in each other's embrace. Ela then let go of Theo, who did the same a few seconds after. He kissed her hand as she left the study. He watched her leave, sighing to himself.

He finished what he was doing, and finished the refreshments Ela brought in. He closed out his computer and left the study. He made sure the flash drive and printed evidence was put into the secret spot before he left.

He entered the living room, seeing Ela read her Bible and write in her journal. He stayed at the entrance just watching her and smiling to himself. He then walked closer to her, as she looked up and smiled.

"What are you reading today, princess?" Theo said, sitting beside her on the couch.

"Ephesians Chapter 1" she said, looking back at her Bible.

"Why don't you read it out loud? That way we can study and use our brains together to better understand it." Theo said, putting his arm on the back of the couch and around her.

Ela started to read Ephesians Chapter one, starting from the beginning, out loud to Theo. She read all twenty three verses, then they talked about the key points, and what they were supposed to learn from the passage. They studied and bounced off ideas to one another, till ten thirty at night.

"Okay, go get you some rest, princess." Theo said, kissing her forehead. He watched her go up the stairs and into her room. He got up off the navy blue-fabric, couch and went upstairs to his room and got ready for bed.

17

Going Back to Normal?

I woke up, exhausted. I slowly sat up in bed. I felt guilty for Theo punishing June. I didn't want any hard feelings or for myself to be the cause. I got up and got dressed in a white floral, short-sleeve puff dress.

I put on some white heels, added a little bit of makeup and fixed my hair. I was gonna try to make things right. I grabbed my purse and walked down the stairs. I sat at the dining table with Edna.

"Good morning, where is Theo?" I asked her.

"He is still asleep, dear," Edna told me, as the maid put food on the table.

"Can you drive me somewhere? But you have to keep it a secret from Theo" I asked the maid.

"Yes ma'am" she said, leaving for the kitchen.

I ate my food and waited. Then we left the house. I gave her the address I wanted to go to. She looked shocked and worried but agreed. We drove all the way over there, I asked her to wait in the car. I got out of the vehicle and went to the entrance. I knocked on the door, to which a maid answered. She let me in and I followed her to where June was sitting.

"June?" I said, stopping a few feet away from her. She looked up, and when she saw me she looked mad.

"What are you doing here? Haven't you done enough" she said, crossing her arms.

"I am not here to cause more trouble or drama. I am here to make things right. What Theo did wasn't exactly right. I never meant to come between you and him." I said. She jumped up from her spot.

"You never meant it? YOU DON'T EVEN KNOW THE HALF OF IT! DID YOU KNOW BEFORE YOU CAME ALONG, HIM AND I WAS SUPPOSED TO GET MARRIED, BUT WHEN YOU CAME ALONG HE CANCELED THE ARRANGED ENGAGEMENT HIS PARENTS SET UP WITH ME! YOU DESTROYED EVERYTHING, MY FUTURE MARRIAGE, MY BUSINESS, MY FRIENDSHIP, EVERYTHING IS GONE BECAUSE OF YOU!" June said.

"Please June," I said, trying to reach out to her.

"NO, YOU SHOULD SUFFER AS MUCH AS I DID!" she said, rushing towards me, raising her hand to slap me.

I shut my eyes tight, bracing myself for the impact. Nothing happened, so I opened my eyes to see Theo standing there, holding her hand, with a mad face. We all froze as he threw her hand away, causing her to sway backwards.

"I thought I told you to leave her alone. Try to put your hands on her again and I will make sure you pay. I will say this one last time, whatever feelings you had towards me, lose them. I don't love you like that. That arranged marriage my parents planned stopped when they died in the car accident years ago, it has nothing to do with Ela. Stay away from me and Ela. Come on Ela, we are leaving" Theo said, grabbing my hand firmly and dragging me out of her house.

We sat there in Theo's car, in silence. He was beyond mad, which he showed on his face. He gripped the steering wheel so tight, while he was driving, that his knuckles were white. I just wanted to make things right, so why do I feel so guilty now?

I started to pray. *'God, help me, I just wanted to do the right thing. What did I do wrong? Is Theo mad at me? God please give me strength and let your will be done. In Your holy name I pray. Amen"*. I watched Theo for a while, even though he didn't say anything. Then I finally got the courage to speak.

"Theo, I'm sorry," I said, trying to lighten the mood.

"Princess, what in your right mind, made you think that was a good idea? You could have gotten hurt. You didn't even tell me where you went and you even told the maid to keep it a secret from me. Do you know how worried I was about you? I had to threaten her job just to get her to tell me where you both were." Theo said, still gripping the wheel tight.

"I am sorry. I just wanted to make things right, and to hopefully clear the misunderstanding." I said, looking down at my folded hands in my lap. Theo sighed.

"I know you had good intentions, but this was not the way to do it. June isn't going to understand because she is prideful and she is jealous. What would you have done if you would have gotten hurt?" Theo said, pulling over in a parking lot.

He parked and looked at me, anger leaving his face and just showing worry and concern. He grabbed my hands and held them. I felt like I couldn't say anything, so I just stayed quiet looking at my hands. He sighed again.

"Princess, look at me," he said, tilting my head over to him so my eyes looked at his. "Don't ever take those kinds of matters into your hands by yourself. I can't stand the thought of ever losing you again. I want to protect you and I can't do that, when you don't tell me things. I am not mad at you, I am mad at myself for not protecting you. I love you Ela," he said.

He kissed my forehead, then turned back to the steering wheel again and started to drive. We rode the rest of the way in silence. When we got home we went inside and I went to the maid immediately and apologized. Theo grabbed my hand afterward and gently dragged me into the study and shut the door.

"Explain the whole plan and everything that happened before I showed up" he said, sitting on the desk in front of me as I stood.

"I wanted to try to fix everything, especially your friendship with her. So I asked the maid to take me over there. When I went over there, she got really mad and started screaming at me, saying I ruined everything for her. Then she came rushing towards me and was about to slap me. That is when you showed up." I said, looking at the floor.

"Princess, look me in the eyes when you talk to me. You don't have to be afraid. Why would you not tell me where you are going or even what you were gonna do?" he asked.

"I was afraid you wouldn't let me go if I told you. I just wanted to help you." I said, doing as he told me. He leaned off of the desk and pulled me into a hug.

"I don't know whether to love that you wear your heart on your sleeve or be worried about it. Thank you for trying to help, princess, but no more pulling dangerous stuff like that. I can take care of both of us, "he said.

"But-" before I could finish my sentence he pulled my head closer and kissed my lips.

All thoughts left my head, as we kissed each other for a little while. He brushed his thumb against my cheek, as he pulled away. We both stared into each other's eyes. Neither one of us dared to break the moment.

He then just stepped back, leaning on his desk again. He put his hands in his pockets as he stared at me. I couldn't figure out what he was thinking. He then smiled at me. He grabbed my hand and pulled me close, holding my waist.

Everything felt like it froze around us. I had my hands on his chest, they landed there when I tried to keep myself from falling. Then a knock came on the door. He let me go smirking and I backed away fast.

Assistant Scott came in holding folders. He looked between the two of us, then a look of realization went across his face. I blushed and left quickly. Theo chuckled and started to talk to his assistant.

I rushed outside into the garden, hoping the fresh air would calm the blush. I took deep breaths. I sat in the chair, in the center of the garden. I took in all of the things God created. I loved being outside in God's creation.

I looked up to the window, where the study is. I noticed Theo watching me. I turned my head away quickly. Why was he watching me? I got my phone out of my purse and got on my devotional app.

I did the lesson there, while I watched the birds and bees fly around. I didn't even notice Edna coming out and sitting beside me. We smiled at each other, while she opened her book. The maid started to do some work on the flower bed.

"Ela dear, I know you are a good girl, but you have to be careful what you do. You are not only representing yourself, but you are representing Theo as well. He has a reputation to keep as well, dear" Edna said.

"Yes ma'am" I said.

She patted my hands and left the garden. I sighed, thinking I caused more trouble than helping. I stood up and walked over to the patch of orchids that Theo said to put in the garden. All I could think was how I was messing everything up for Theo.

I started to walk through the garden, just thinking. All of a sudden, two arms wrapped around my waist and pulled me back. When I tried to struggle, I smelled a familiar cologne. I looked over my shoulder, Theo smiled while laying his head on my shoulder.

"What are you doing, princess?" He asked.

"Thinking" I said, leaning back into his hold.

"What's the matter?" he said.

"Did I ruin your reputation with my actions today?" I asked, feeling sad.

"No, princess. You had good intentions, and reporters were nowhere near so nobody even knew but us." Theo said, letting me go and grabbing his phone from his pocket. He turned on some music and placed his phone on a brick. "Would you care to dance, my lady?"

"Of course," I said, taking his hand.

We began to dance to the slow music. He would twirl me, and we talked and laughed. We danced for an hour. Enjoying ourselves and our moment together. At the end of the song, he twirled me towards him, and lifted my chin. We kissed, and it felt like time stopped once more.

"I've got a reservation booked with the restaurant we like. We are gonna leave in thirty minutes. Go get ready with Grandma." Theo said, kissing me on my cheek then letting me go.

"Okay" I said, and started to walk away, I then came back to him, grabbed him by his tie and pulled him down, then I kissed his cheek and walked away.

Thirty minutes later, we were ready and left the house. We arrived at the restaurant and went in. We sat at the VIP section and ordered our food. Edna started to talk to Theo about the company.

"Princess?" Theo asked, bringing me back from my thoughts.

"Yes?" I asked. He chuckled.

"I asked if you would attend the award show with me, about three weeks from now," he said.

"Oh, sure. Sounds like fun" I said, embarrassed I wasn't paying attention.

"What's the matter?" He asked.

"Nothing, just thinking about the center and the animals." I said.

"Don't worry, they are fine, we hired a worker to help you when you can't be there," he said, as the food arrived.

He blessed the food and we ate. Edna got spaghetti, Theo got an eight ounce ribeye with a sweet potato and salad, and I also got the eight ounce ribeye but with sweet potato fries and a salad. We ate our food in peace, till close to the end.

June came to the table, asking to speak with Theo alone. He looked towards me and I shrugged. He reluctantly accepted and excused himself from the table. He followed her outside. We watched them leave.

I started to feel a pang of jealousy in my heart, but pushed it away. I knew he wouldn't do anything to hurt me, but something was telling me something bad would happen. I didn't want to intrude on their conversation, but something was telling me to check.

I excused myself from the table and went towards the direction they went. I went outside, and looked to my left, then my right. My heart dropped and tears started to run down my face. Edna came out with our bags and looked where I was looking. She was furious.

I grabbed my purse that she handed me and turned around and started running. I heard her call after me, but I couldn't stay. I didn't know where I was going, and at the moment I didn't care. I just wanted to be away from all of that.

I don't know how long I ran, just that I ended up at a huge park and the sun was going down. I couldn't stop asking questions and thinking about what happened. Why did they do that? Why would he cheat? Was I not good enough? What am I gonna do now? Where would I stay?

I managed to calm down and talk to God. 'Lord, I don't know what to do. I am scared. What is going to happen to me? Why would he do that?-'. Before I could finish my conversation with God someone called out my name.

"Ela?" the person said. I looked up.

"Avery? Liam?" I asked. They sat beside me.

"What are you doing out here alone? Especially in the dark as well? Where is Theo?" They asked. Tears started to flow down my face once again.

"Theo was kissing June," I said, trying to stop the tears.

"Wait what? This isn't right. Explain what happened." Liam said. So I did, I told them everything that happened since we arrived at the restaurant.

"Okay, that really doesn't sound like something Theo would do, but you can come live with us, until we figure out what is going on." Avery said. They walked me to their car, and took me to their house.

18

Misunderstanding and Looking for Her

Theo pushed June off of him as Ela ran away. Edna slapped June, as June smirked and walked off.

"What in the world do you think you are doing? Do you know how much you just messed up? Do you know how hurt Ela is right now?" Edna said, fuming.

"Grandma, it's a misunderstanding. She kissed me, I didn't kiss her back, I was trying to push her off of me. Please believe me. Where is Ela?" Theo kept saying.

"She is gone, She saw you do that and stormed off upset. You need to get your act straight. I did not raise you like this. If she saw it the way I did, she would more than likely not forgive you, and at this point I wouldn't blame her." Edna said, starting to walk away.

"Grandma, please forgive me. Please tell me where she went," Theo said, starting to tear up.

"Even if I knew, which I don't. Do you really think finding her will help?" Edna asked.

"Please," Theo begged.

"She went that way, but I don't know where she went after that. Don't mess it up even more." Edna said, pointing in the direction Ela went.

Theo took off running in that direction. He searched as much as he could, looking down every alley and in every building. He ran searching for a few miles till he ended up at a park. He sat on a bench and ran his finger through his hair. He then got his phone and started to dial Liam's number.

"Hello?" Liam said.

"Dude, I need your help. I messed up and Ela ran away. I can't find her. I need your help. Please" Theo begged his friend.

"Dude, relax, meet me at the cafe in thirty minutes. You can tell me what happened, I assure you, she is safe" Liam said, hanging up the phone.

Theo stood up and walked towards the cafe. He went in and found a table and waited for his friend. His leg shook with anxiousness while he waited. He then saw Liam walk in the entrance. Liam came walking to the table.

"Ok, tell me what happened and explain in detail" Liam said.

"We were eating at the restaurant when June walked in and asked to speak to me alone. I obliged and followed her out. She started to explain that she was sorry for her actions earlier. Then all of a sudden, she looked at the restaurant door, then she grabbed my shirt and pulled me closer, forcibly kissing me. I pushed her away immediately. The next thing I know, Grandma slapped her. Grandma said Ela ran off when she saw it. I messed up, and now I can't even find her to explain and make things right." Theo explained.

"Did you ever think she did it because she knew Ela was gonna check on you. She knew she could drive you away from each other?" Liam said, taking a sip of coffee.

"I don't know, but please, you have to help me find her. I can't lose her again, she means too much to me." Theo begged.

"Relax. She is safe. I am not gonna tell you where she is, though." Liam said, putting a hand up.

"Please Liam. Please let me go to her and see her," Theo kept begging.

"No. If you really care about her, one you are gonna have to prove it and two what you did is all over the news. You are gonna have to deal with that first." Liam said, showing Theo his phone.

"It is all over the internet– that you cheated on Ella with your childhood ex-fiance" Liam said, as Theo watched the video and photos.

"Obviously I am being framed. What do I need to do?" Theo asked, after the video finished.

"You are gonna have to figure that out yourself. Theo you messed up. You have to fix your mistakes. You need to own up to what you did. You shouldn't have even followed her out. You should have stayed with Ela and just told her to say what she needed to say. Ela is in a safe place, so don't worry about her" Liam said, standing from the table.

Theo sighed and ran his hand through his hair. He stood up as well and walked out of the cafe with Liam. He told Liam bye and dialed his assistant on his phone.

"Send a car to pick me up at the cafe and get a press conference ready for me this afternoon" Theo said.

The car came a few minutes later. He climbed in and headed to the company. He waited an hour in the company getting his notes together, then headed to the press conference. He walked on the stage, while cameras flashed.

"Thank you for coming to this press conference today. I am doing this because there are some rumors going around the internet saying I cheated on Ela with June. I am here to clarify, I did not cheat. We were eating at the restaurant when June came to our table and asked if she could speak to me in private. I was dumb. I agreed and followed her outside. She started to apologize that she didn't mean to do her actions. She saw Ela coming out of the restaurant then grabbed my shirt and forcibly kissed me. I pushed her away immediately. I did not kiss her back. The reason why my hands were on her arms, was that I was trying to push her away from me without hurting her. I do not have any feelings towards June. Ela is the one I love, She is the one I want to marry, nobody else. I love Ela with all of my heart and I want to always love and protect her. I messed up, because I followed June out of the restaurant. I should have known it would be one of the traps to break me and Ela up. This is the truth I wanted to spread. If you would take a look at the screen, I have Junes bank account record showing that she paid paparazzi. She even has an email saying where to meet and when to take the pictures. All of this was to frame me and to try to break me and Ela up. Ela, princess if you are watching this, I didn't cheat on you, I love you with all of my heart, please forgive me. Thank you" Theo said, then walking off of the stage.

Reporters started to whisper as cameras kept flashing. Theo walked to the back of the stage and sighed. Hopefully that is enough to fix things. He got his phone out and tried to call Ela again, it just went to voicemail. He then texted Liam, asking if he could please tell him where Ela was.

When Liam told him no, Theo snapped, he went back to the company and changed into his spy outfit. If his friends wouldn't help, he would find her himself. He started researching locations and pinging her last known location.

He found her. He left the company and got in his black jeep. He rode to Liam's house, determined to see her. He arrived at Liam's house and knocked on the door. Liam answered looking surprised then annoyed.

"What are you doing here, Theo?" Liam asked, crossing his arms.

"Let me see her, I know she is here." Theo demanded.

"She is here, but you are not seeing her. Not right now, you need to let things calm down" Liam said.

"Liam, I am not going to say it again, LET… ME… SEE HER." Theo demanded.

"Theo, I am not scared of you, she isn't ready to see you, go home and let things calm down." Liam said, shutting the door in Theo's face.

Theo fist his hands and walked around the house, knowing the cameras saw him, he didn't care. He knew where their guest bedroom was and climbed the tree and in through the window. He was determined to get Ela back.

He hid in the closet and waited for her to come in and go to bed. He watched her lay in bed after turning the lights out, he waited and then came out of the closet. He covered her mouth, keeping her from screaming.

"Shhhhhh, it's me, don't scream, don't let them know I am in here, I will release you, just don't scream" Theo whispered, as she mumbled against his hand. She calmed down and he let go.

"Why are you here, Theo?" She asked in a sad whisper.

"I am here for you, I came to take you back." Theo said, sitting beside her on the bed.

"No, Theo. I am not going back there. Go live your life with your fiance" she said.

"There is no fiance, I don't love her Ela, I only love you. You are my one and only, she forced herself on me, I tried to push her away without hurting her" Theo said.

Ela stayed silent. She looked away from him. He sighed and tilted her face to his. He rubbed her cheek with his thumb, while staring at her eyes. He then kissed her forehead and hugged her. She tried to struggle out of his grasp. Then all of a sudden the door burst open and Liam walked in and dragged him off of her.

"I will prove to you that I am innocent, I LOVE YOU ELA!" Theo said, as Liam pushed him out of the room. Liam pushed him all the way out of the entrance.

"You have gone too far, man. I know you work for us, but I am not afraid to take you to the station, go home and stop this" Liam said, once again shutting the door in Theo's face. Liam then made sure all windows were locked and all doors were locked.

19

Sadness and Lost Trust

I watched as Liam took Theo away, Avery came to check on me. I gave her a sad smile as she sat on the bed with me. I leaned my head on her shoulder. I love Theo, but I was so hurt by what I saw. That I didn't know if I could ever forgive him.

Avery handed me her Bible, and showed me some Bible verses on forgiveness and other things. I read Mark 11:25, Ephesians 4:32, Matthew 6:15, James 5:16, Luke 6:37, and Colossians 3:13.

I hugged her and then she went to bed. I went to bed as well. I felt sad that I was pushing Theo away, but my heart couldn't take it anymore. I really do love Theo, but I didn't want to be hurt anymore.

I drifted off to sleep, tossing and turning most of the night. I woke up the next morning, thanked God for waking me up and giving me the strength to get ready. I went down and met Liam and Avery in the kitchen.

Liam handed me a cup of coffee, which I gladly accepted. I smiled at them as they talked. Their love was so evident, and it just made me feel like I was intruding. I looked at Avery who looked at me.

"Can I use your Bible to study for a little bit?" I asked her.

"Sure, but are you not going to wait for the food?" She asked.

"No thank you, I am not hungry" I said, as she handed me her Bible.

I took her Bible and my coffee into their living room. I sat down and started to read different verses on sadness, hurt, and trust.

Then I talked to God for a while. I knew whatever God's plan was, it would happen.

"Hey Ela, we have to go to the station today. Are you gonna be okay by yourself?" Avery asked.

"Yeah, I will be fine. Go do your jobs" I said.

"We will keep the doors and windows locked, so he won't be able to come in. You will be safe here" Liam said.

"Thanks" I said, giving them a smile.

They left and I was left in their house, all alone. I sighed and got up. I grabbed my phone out of my purse, plugged it up and turned it on. I looked at all of the missed calls and messages from Theo. My heart hurt.

I read each one. Tears started to flow down my face. Then I got a notification he was going live. I clicked on it and watched it live. He was apologizing to me and explaining what happened. I cried more.

Have I really misunderstood him? I looked on Google and saw the press conference he held yesterday. I watched the video. Oh no, I pushed him away when he was trying to explain and apologize.

I texted him after I calmed down. *I just saw the live and the press conference. I forgive you and I love you too. Let's meet at the park where you introduced me to Liam and Avery.* I sent the message. Immediately he responded saying *okay*.

I got dressed in the clothes I wore yesterday. I packed everything up and wrote a little note for Avery and Theo. I unlocked the door and then locked it back. I walked to the park. When I arrived I saw him pacing.

"Theo?" I said. He looked towards me and ran to me, embracing me into a hug. I hugged him back.

"I'm so, so sorry you had to go through that yesterday. I love you so much princess" Theo said.

"I love you too. It's fine. I know what happened now" I said. We stayed in the hug for a while.

"Let's go back home now" Theo said, letting go of the hug.

"Mhm, okay" I said.

He grabbed my hand and led me to his car. We rode back home and finally arrived. We went inside. Edna saw us and came and hugged me.

"Oh, dear I am so glad you are back" she said, I hugged her back

"I'm sorry I ran off like that. I am back now and I forgive him" I said, as he came to hold my hand.

"This calls for a celebratory dinner. I will get the maid to start on it" Edna said, excited.

I giggled at her as she made her way into the kitchen. I went to change into some fresh clothes. Then I came back down and noticed Theo was talking on the phone. I came up from behind him and hugged him.

He hung up and put his hands on my arms. He chuckled and turned around. He pulled me tighter into a hug. We stayed in the hug, till the maid came to get us. We then went to the dining room and sat down. We blessed the food and ate.

They made sweet potato fries, spaghetti, fried squash, fried green tomatoes, and rolls. It was so good. We finished our food, then went into the garden. Theo played music on his phone again and we danced again.

We stayed in the garden, just enjoying each other's company and talking about God. We then went inside and watched a movie in the living room. It felt really good to be by his side once again.

My phone buzzed and I picked it up and looked at it. Avery had texted me. 'Glad you and Theo made up. We knew he wasn't a bad guy, he just had to fix his mistakes'. I smiled as I read that. I replied back to her. 'yeah me too. I am glad God had a plan all along'.

I put my phone down as I watched Theo. He noticed me staring at him and looked at me and smiled. I smiled back at him. He tilted my chin up like he always did and leaned in, we kissed each other.

As the sun went down, we finished the movie. Then we went upstairs to get ready for bed. I laid down wondering what God had planned in the future. I fell asleep not long after. I woke up early the next morning, and took a shower.

I got ready for the day. Then I went down the stairs. I couldn't find Theo in the living room so I went to his study. I noticed he was in there talking on the phone. I went silently in and stood at the door. He noticed me and motioned for me to come in. I walked in and sat in the chair across from his desk. He hung up the phone a few minutes later.

"Good morning, princess. What are you doing up so early?" he said.

"I wanted to get some stuff done. What are you doing?" I said, fiddling with the fidget toy he had on his desk.

"Working on some things, trying to get other companies to merge together, that will be going out of business soon" Theo said.

"I just wanted to see, when you get the chance, if you could take me to the center. So I could work with the animals today?" I asked.

"Yeah, I got to go to the company anyway. I can drop you off on my way there. Let's go" he said, gathering his stuff and taking my hand.

I put my purse on my shoulder and followed him out. He dropped me off at the building and kissed my forehead, before he left. I went in and unlocked the door. I remembered Theo talked about a person who came by here about twice a day to take care of the animals.

I turned on the lights and noticed a few more animals had been surrendered. There was a gerbil, guinea pig, and a tarantula had been surrendered. I fed everything and made sure water dishes were filled.

Then I made sure all enclosures were clean. I checked on the rehab animals to make sure they were doing good. I then cleaned around the center and checked emails. One email stuck out to me.

'I have a baby sulcata tortoise. It hasn't been eating for me and I don't know what to do. Can you please take it?'

I replied to the email saying to go ahead and bring it over. I prepared the exam table for it. I fixed some kale and other greens for it to try to eat when it arrives. Then I got a container to put it in temporarily.

The woman arrived with the tortoise and I let her fill out a form, then put the information into the system. I took it to the back and examined it. Everything looked normal, so then I offered it the food. It took the food no problem.

I got a little feeder bin, stuck it in the corner, near the adoption part. Then I put coconut fiber substrate in the bin. I put a hide, heat lamp, food and water dish in the bin as well. I put some twigs and pebbles for enrichment in there as well.

I filled the water dish and then put the baby tortoise into it. I continued to check on the baby sugar glider, I was worried as it continued to be lethargic. I finished up my work and got picked up by Theo, who was wearing his spy outfit.

"What happened, why are you in that outfit?" I asked him.

"Hmmm, oh it is nothing" he said, focusing on the road.

I was skeptical so I reached out to him, and pulled his mask off of his face. He had bruises and cuts all over his face. I gasped and rubbed my finger against the wounds.

"What happened" I said, he sighed.

"Someone we caught while trying to get a confession out of, decided to try to escape and fight back," he said.

When we arrived home, I grabbed his hands and rushed him inside. I told him to sit in the living room. I went to get the first aid kit. I started to clean the wounds on his face, then put medicine on it.

Then I noticed his hand was bleeding. I cleaned the cut and put medicine on it as well and bandaged it. I cleaned up the mess and sat on the floor in front of him. He looked distant again. I reached out and gently put my hand on his cheek.

He jumped out of his thoughts and focused on me. He took my hand in his, and moved his mouth closer to my open hand. He gave small kisses on it. He then leaned on my shoulder.

20

The Awards Show

Two weeks have passed and it was time for the awards show. Theo got ready in a black sequined tux. He slicked his hair back and looked at himself in the mirror. He was nervous, because he had something special planned for Ela.

He finished getting ready and headed downstairs. He didn't see Ela as she was still getting ready. He saw his grandmother talking to the maid. He walked over, but then heard heels clacking upstairs.

He looked up and saw Ela coming down. She wore a gorgeous modest navy blue sequin dress. Theo stood there, amazed and in shock. His mind thinks how beautiful she is.

"Do you like it?" Ela asked him.

"I love it, you look absolutely beautiful" Theo said, grabbing her hand. "Are you ready to go?"

"Yes" she said, as they walked out of the entrance with Edna.

They got a limo Theo rented and headed off to the award ceremony, as Assistant Scott drove the limo. Ela pushed her curled hair past her shoulders and out of her face. Theo watched her, feeling completely in love.

They arrived at the ceremony and got out. They walked down the carpet as the cameras flashed their pictures. They walked in the entrance of the building and Theo started talking to people he knew, while Ela held onto his arm. Edna walked further in with Assistant Scott.

"How are you Mr. Chan?" Theo asked the older looking man.

"Good, how are you? And who is this beautiful lady?" Mr. Chan said

"I am good. This is my girlfriend, Ela" Theo said, smiling.

"Well you sure are lucky, Mr. Ambrose" Mr. Chan said.

"Yes, I am. We will see you later" Theo said, walking and guiding Ela away.

"Are you ok? I know this can be an uncomfortable environment if you are not used to it." Theo asked Ela.

"Mhm, I am fine, I have you and God by my side" Ela said.

They both smiled at each other and kept walking. Occasionally stopping to talk. They made their way to their seats and sat down. The lights dimmed and spotlights showed on stage. A person in a white suit came out and started talking into a microphone.

"Ladies and gentlemen, thank you for coming to the fourth annual awards ceremony. Let's get started shall we?" The man said.

There were several people getting awards. Men and women going up to claim theirs. Theo held Ela's hand the entire time. The ceremony went on for five hours. Then came the last award for the day.

"Ladies and gentlemen, our last award for the day, The CEO of the year award. And the award goes to… Theo Ambrose!" The man said.

Theo stood from his chair. He made his way onto the stage. He accepted the award and shook the man's hand. He was thinking to God 'Lord is this the right moment to do this?'. He made his way to the microphone, and as he did, he felt God tell him yes.

"Thank you so much for nominating me for this award. It means alot with how much work I put into the company. I will gladly accept this award, but there is something else I want to do as well. All of you know me and who I am, you also know my girlfriend, Ela. I want to ask Ela up on the stage with me. Ela, Will you come up here?" Theo said, as the crowd started to cheer. Ela made her way up on the stage.

"Ela, We have been together for about five months now. We have also been through our fights and problems. Ela I want to ask. Will you marry me?" Theo said, getting on one knee and holding a navy blue box with a square shaped diamond ring. Everyone gasped and went quiet, waiting for her answer.

"Yes!" Ela said, hugging Theo.

Theo hugged her back, then put the ring on her finger. Theo then kissed her, as camera's started to flash. They parted from each other, and walked off the stage. They sat back in their seats. Edna is ecstatic about the good news.

"Well, ladies and gentlemen, that was quite a show. Was it not? Congratulations to the happy couple. Hope all goes well. That is all for today, folks. Have a good day," the man said.

Everyone started to get up and leave. Theo stood up with Edna, then looked at Ela and chuckled. She was mesmerized by the ring on her finger, not even paying attention. Theo extended his hand in front of her.

"Are you ready to go, princess?" Theo asked, smiling.

Ela looked away from the ring and up towards him. She nodded and took his hand. They all walked out together. Cameras still flashed as they left the building. They make their way back to the limo and Assistant Scott goes the opposite way from their home.

"Where are we going?" Ela asked.

"I have another surprise for you." Theo said, smiling while holding her hand.

They rode for about fifteen minutes, then made it to the park. They got out of the limo and went into the entrance of the park. When they arrived at the big cherry blossom tree, they saw Liam and Avery standing there.

They started clapping and congratulating the two. Theo was so happy. He grabbed Ela by her waist and pulled her close, as he talked to Liam. Avery was also pulled close by Liam. They talked for a while, then Avery got tired so Liam took her home. Theo and Ela were left there alone. Theo got his phone out and started to play music. As the sun set, Theo held out his hand in front of Ela

"Care to dance, my lady?" Theo asked.

Ela giggled and took his hand. They began to dance to the slow music beside the cherry blossom tree. Music filled the cold air. They danced and just enjoyed each other's company. Eventually the sun went down, so they headed back to the entrance.

They made their way back home. They arrived and Edna looked up from her book, as she relaxed in the living room. They went close to the stairs. Ela turned back to Theo.

"Get some rest, princess. Sweet dreams." Theo said, kissing her forehead.

He watched her go upstairs. Then he sat beside Edna and loosened his tie. He stared at the award on the coffee table. Two accomplishments in one day. He thought that was crazy. He got his Bible and started to study.

"Well, are you happy now? You got what you wanted." Edna asked her grandson.

"Mhm, I am. I am very happy she forgave me and accepted. Now we just have to keep June away from us and especially her. I figure it won't take long for the reporters to have the news spread by morning." Theo said.

21

Engaged and a Surprise

I woke up the next morning, feeling something on my finger. I jolted up, then looked down. I then remembered everything that happened yesterday. Theo proposed and I accepted. I stared at the ring.

I finally decided to just get up and get ready. I put on a pink modest dress with some wedges. I finished getting ready then headed downstairs. I saw everyone seated at the table, so I sat down. The maid put food in front of me, and I blessed my food.

"So, when are you two gonna start the wedding planning?" Edna asked. We looked at each other and blushed.

"Grandma, it might be a little too early for that just yet. We just got engaged yesterday." Theo said.

"Nonsense, me and your grandfather got married four months after being engaged. Don't worry dear, I will give you some books to help you out" Edna said.

I just smiled and nodded. I kept eating, as Theo sighed and shook his head, but I noticed his smile on his face. It made me smile too. I finished my food while they talked and excused myself from the table.

I went outside to the garden, with my phone and Bible. I did the devotional app then read the first chapter of Revelation. Then I prayed and just enjoyed God's presence. Then Theo came outside.

"Hey princess, we got to go. Avery is in labor and might be having her baby today" Theo said.

"Okay, I am coming" I said, as I stood up and grabbed my stuff.

I followed him back into the living room, put my stuff down and grabbed my purse. I then took his outstretched hand and walked with him to his Bugatti. We got in and started the drive towards the hospital. We arrived at the hospital and met Liam in the waiting room.

"Hey, they are checking her vitals, then they will give her an epidural and she will start having the baby girl soon" Liam said.

"That is great. Go be with your wife. We will wait here till she has her." Theo said, pulling Ela by the waist closer to him.

"Okay, I will come get you guys in a little bit" Liam said, then turned to go back to the delivery room.

We went and sat in the waiting room. Theo held my hand as we waited. I kept staring at the ring on my finger. Wondering what it would be like, to be married and to have a kid. Theo noticed I was lost in thought, so he tilted my chin towards him and kissed me.

"It's gonna be ok, she is a fighter. She will make it through this." Theo said, I nodded.

We waited for two hours, then Liam came into the waiting room. Panting but looking happy he smiled when he found us.

"Come on back, guys. Come meet the baby girl." Liam said. We followed him to the room. Avery saw us and told us to come in.

"Guys, meet Bella Rose Smith" Avery said, holding the baby.

"She's beautiful," I said.

"You did good, Avery," Theo said.

"Ela, do you want to hold her?" Avery asked.

"Oh, um I … I don't know how." I said.

"It's ok, Theo can teach you. Here you go" she said, handing her over with Theo's help.

I was holding the little girl in my hands. I was so nervous that I would drop her, but with Theo's help I wasn't scared. We held her in our arms, she looked just like Avery. Then without warning, tears started to flow.

"Ela, princess, what's wrong?" Theo asked.

"Nothing… Thank you for letting me hold her. I'm sorry I ruined the mood." I said, handing the baby back to Avery and walking out of the room. Theo followed behind me and grabbed my arm and pulled me close.

"Princess, what's wrong? Please tell me." Theo said.

"It's nothing… Just in the past, I would have been like her." I said.

"I am not following." Theo said, with a confused look.

"Back when I lived with Vincent, he had gotten me pregnant. But when he found out, he beat me, and I lost the baby." I said, tears flowing heavier.

"Oh, princess, I'm so sorry" Theo said, pulling me into his arms again, comforting me. "Don't think about it anymore. You are no longer with him. He can't ever hurt you anymore. Plus the way he starved you, you are blessed by God that you are still even alive right now. Let's go back, before they feel bad that they did something wrong, ok?"

"Mhm" I said. We went back into the room.

"Hey, is everything okay?" Avery asked.

"Yeah, I'm better now. Don't worry," I said.

We stayed for a little while, holding and watching the baby. Then visiting hours were over, so we left to let them rest. We went back home and I was about to go upstairs to my room, when Theo pulled me back into his arms.

"Not so fast princess. We need to talk, let's go to the balcony" he said, guiding me to the balcony.

"Ok, now I know this is hard for you to talk about, but I need to know what happened to you so I can continue to protect and comfort you. Can you do that for me?" Theo asked.

I nodded and told him everything that happened, from the time I could remember to the day I was sold. It was hard but he comforted me every step of the way. Eventually the sun went down, and we were just hugging for comfort.

"I am so sorry that happened to you Princess. But now I know I can help you. I also know, he can never hurt you again, or lay a hand on you ever again. I love you princess, I will always protect you from now on" Theo said.

He then gave me a kiss on my forehead and guided me back inside as it was getting a bit chilly. We went down into the living room and started to do a Bible study. We read Revelation 21:4, Psalms 34:18, John 16:22, Matthew 5:4, Isaiah 41:10, and Psalms 147:3. My heart felt at peace then.

We then got ready for bed. I lay down and prayed to God again. "Lord, thank you for everything. Lord, I know you had a plan for all those horrible things that happened to me. Thank you for the new strength you have given me."

22

Justice Is Served

Theo woke up the next morning. He got up and got ready. Then he checked on Ela, who was still asleep. He grabbed his phone and went into his study and closed the door. He made a phone call to Liam.

"Hey, I know you are enjoying your time with your wife and baby, but I have more evidence against Vincent. You might want to have a listen to Ela's full story." Theo said, holding the recorder in his hand.

Theo didn't want to trick Ela, but he needed all he could get to take Vincent down. He prayed. "Lord, help me to bring justice for Ela. She deserves happiness. She deserves to feel safe. Help us to bring this evil man down, Lord."

He put the recorder in his pocket and made a note for Ela, for when she wakes up. 'I had some business to take care of, go ahead and eat with Grandma. I will be back soon'. He left the note on the table and left the house. He met Liam in the hospital parking lot.

"Here you go, Ela's full story. Take this man down once and for all." Theo said.

"I will give this to the sheriff when he visits. How is Ela? I know she was upset yesterday" Liam said.

"She is fine, How is Avery and Bella?" Theo asked.

"They are fine, Avery is just exhausted," Liam said. "Anyways thanks for this, It will get it taken care of" he said, walking back into the hospital.

Theo walked back to his Mustang. When he got in he sighed. Then he started the car and went back home. He arrived home and went inside. He saw Ela and his grandmother talking in the living room.

"Hey" Ela said, standing up.

"Good morning princess" Theo said, grabbing her into a hug, and placing his head on her shoulder.

"What's wrong?" She asked

"Nothing, it's fine, it's just been a long morning already. Did you eat?" Theo said.

"Mhm, we had eggs and bacon and toast. If you are hungry, the maid can get your plate and heat it back up, "she said.

"Nah it is fine. Not hungry right now. Lets just sit and watch a movie, how about that?" Theo said.

"Sure," Ela said.

They sat beside Edna and turned the TV on. They watched a Christian movie for a while. Assistant Scott came in and Theo followed him into the study. They closed the door, and looked at the folders Scott had.

"What do you got?" Theo said.

"The evidence you sent to Liam and the sheriff. They took it and will use it against Vincent and his friends. The only problem is, the courts want Ela to be there to testify against them as well" Assistant Scott said.

"They can't just use that, which was given to them. She is literally the one telling the story" Theo said.

"Afraid not, she has to be present there and testify that the story is true. What do you want to do?" Scott said.

"Okay, I will talk to her, and try to make her understand that what was done was necessary and for her to be there," Theo said, sighing.

They left the study and walked back into the living room. They saw Ela and Edna talking. Scott gave Theo a half smile then left the house. Theo walked over to Ela and grabbed her hand.

"Princess, I need to talk to you in private." Theo said.

"Okay?" Ela said, standing up and letting Theo guide her into the study. Theo closed the door after they walked in.

"Princess, you are probably gonna be mad at me, and you have every right to be. Do you remember when you told me your past?" Theo said.

"Yeah, what's going on, Theo?" Ela said, crossing her arms.

"I recorded your story and took it to the sheriff. They took the evidence and are gonna pin it against Vincent and his friends, but they want you to be present in court to testify that the story is true" Theo said, leaning on his desk, watching every emotion cross Ela's face.

"Theo… Why would you even do that without asking me? I trusted you." Ela said.

"I know, and I should have asked you, but I knew you wouldn't tell the full story if you knew I was recording you. I did this to protect you princess." Theo said, coming closer to her.

"By giving something I wanted kept secret to the police for them to play it infront of a bunch of people, and now you're telling me I have to say it is true in front of those people including the people who hurt me!? Why?" Ela said, tearing up.

"I'm sorry princess. I did something stupid again, but it is for the best. We can finally put those jerks behind bars" Theo said.

"I'm sorry. Theo you betrayed me, I thought I could trust you. I can't do that" Ela said, walking out of the study.

"Princess!" Theo said after her.

He watched her leave, upset. He was mad at himself for not talking to her, and even more so for making her cry and hurting her. He sighed and sat at his desk, running his hand through his hair.

"WHAT DID YOU DO!?" Edna came into the study, mad. "Why did Ela just run out of the house so upset? What did you do this time?"

"I'm sorry Grandma. I messed up, again." Theo said.

"Yeah, you did. Whatever you did, she might not forgive you so easily this time." Edna said.

"What do you mean?" Theo asked

"She took her ring off and left it on the counter as she stormed out. Probably serves you right. If you can't treat her right, you are no better than the people who hurt her in her past." Edna said, placing the ring on his desk and left the study.

"What have I done? She hates me now." Theo said, picking up the ring and looking at it. He moved the ring between his fingers.

He picked up his phone and called his assistant. "Give me everything you can find about Ela. Dig deep and do a full background check of everything".

23

Overthinking

I stormed out, so upset I could barely think. How could he go behind my back and do that to me? How could he expect me to do that? Why wouldn't he ask me before he did that? Why did he keep it a secret?

I walked for so long, repeating those questions in my head, I didn't even realize I had walked all the way into town. I tried to get out of my thoughts. Luckily, I grabbed my purse when I left. I walked into a small cafe and ordered a coffee.

I sat at a corner table with my coffee and stared out of the window. I still repeated those questions over and over again in my head. I couldn't understand why he would do that. I messed with the throw away cup, as I watched people walk and talk down the street.

What am I doing? Why am I even being like this? He said he was trying to protect me, why can't I believe him? Why is it so hard to trust him right now? All he has ever done was help me. I sighed and got my phone out of my purse.

I pulled up the Bible app and read some verses on trust. I read 1 John 4:18, Proverbs 3:5, Psalms 56:3, and Psalms 40:4. I then began to pray, knowing God has a plan for everything, and that I trust him.

When I got done praying I felt more at peace. The only thing to figure out is what I am going to do now. I only had 250 dollars cash left over. Could I go back to the house? Would they accept me back?

I stared at my finger where the engagement ring used to be. Did I overreact back there? Did I do the wrong thing blowing up at him?

Would he forgive me for blowing up at him? I stared at the cup in my hands.

"Ela?" a familiar voice said, I looked up and saw June standing there.

"June?" I said, surprised to see her, I immediately hid my hands.

"What are you doing here? Where is Theo?" June asked.

"Oh, um I wanted to enjoy some time to myself." I said. Which wasn't a lie, but she didn't need to know the details.

"Well it is good you are by yourself. I wanted to talk to you. May I sit?" June said, motioning towards the chair across from me.

"Sure" I said, she did.

"I wanted to formally and sincerely apologize to you. My actions from before were not acceptable. Since you are now going to be Mrs. Ambrose soon, there is no sense of me trying to fight or be jealous of you anymore. You won. I hope you make each other happy." June said.

"Thank you, I accept your apology." I said. Just then Theo came into the cafe and looked at us both.

"June, you better not be trying to start any more trouble," Theo said, Grabbing my hand.

"No, Theo, she was apologizing. Everything is good, no trouble" I said, putting my free hand on his arm to calm him down.

"Good, come on, let's go." Theo said, as I grabbed my purse.

"Thank you for apologizing again" I said, as we exited the cafe.

I followed him to his car and got in. There was a long silence for a little while. I saw he was messing with the engagement ring. I looked down at my hands.

"I'm sorry" we both said at the same time. We stared at each other.

"What are you sorry for? I am the one who broke your trust." Theo said.

"I'm sorry I blew up at you like I did and stormed out. I should have listened to you and communicated better with you" I said.

"That should be my line." Theo said, chuckling.

"Do you forgive me princess, and be my fiance again?" He asked, holding the ring out to me.

"Yes" I said, letting him put the ring back on my ring finger. I smiled at it again, feeling right for it to be back on.

"Let's go home, princess," Theo said.

I agreed and we rode back home. We arrived and noticed Edna and the maid talking. Edna and I hugged when we walked in the living room. I felt happy to be back at the place I actually felt I belonged.

"Theo… I will testify at the court." I said, turning to him.

"Are you sure? You don't have to. We can find other evidence to bring in front of the judge." Theo said.

"I am sure. If it gets him out of my life for good. I will do anything to make sure he is behind bars" I said.

"Ok, it is in a few days. I will be right beside you the whole time." Theo said.

"Mhm" I said.

Theo went into his study. I went into the garden with Edna. We talked and enjoyed being in the garden. Edna was called in by the maid after a while. I stayed in the garden and sat in the chair. The maid brought my devotional books to me.

I started to read and write in those books. I spent time with God, which felt awesome to be in his presence again. I did a bunch of different devotionals and lessons. The wind blew slightly, but not hard enough that I couldn't handle it.

I heard footsteps approaching from behind me. I turned my head and looked up to see Theo and Scott coming out to the garden. We smiled at each other. I stood up, my dress blowing slightly from the wind. Theo smiled and took his suit jacket off. He placed the jacket on my shoulders.

"Don't catch a cold. Wear this" he said.

"Ok" I said, while nodding.

"Want to take a walk through the garden?" Theo asked.

"Sure," I said.

We started to walk through the enormous garden of different varieties of flowers. I was so mesmerized by the peacefulness of the walk, I didn't realize he grabbed my hand at first, until he pulled me closer to him. Embracing me with a hug.

"I am so blessed God gave me you" he said, which made me blush.

"Me too," I said. We stayed in the hug for a little bit.

All of a sudden gunshots rang out in the distance. Theo pushed me to the ground gently, with his body covering me, protecting me. He searched the surroundings with his eyes. Staying quiet so as to not give away where we are.

Theo put an earpiece in his ear. He started to give off commands into the earpiece. A few minutes later, some of Theo's masked men showed up. They got in front of us and acted like a shield, with guns raised high and ready. Theo stood up and picked me up bridal style.

I clung to him, shaking, as he quickly carried me into the house. He carried me to the study and pressed a button, which opened a secret room. He carried me into the room, Edna and the maid were already seated there.

"Stay in here. This room will keep you safe. No one else knows about this room" Theo said, setting me down in a chair.

"What about you?" I said, grabbing his sleeve as he tried to leave.

"Don't worry, princess. I will be fine, I am gonna help my men defend you and the place. But don't worry, I am not gonna kill anyone. The guns we use are tranquilizers. We don't shoot to kill. Stay safe princess, I will be back to get you." Theo said, kissing me before leaving and closing the hidden room off.

We could still hear gunshots in the distance. '*Lord, please protect Theo. Give him strength to be able to protect us all. I pray he makes it out okay.*' I sent a prayer up, worried but knowing God has got us.

The gunfight lasted an hour, then all went quiet. We stayed inside, trying to listen intently to what was happening outside. Then we heard Theo talking to his men, to clean up the mess, and take the knocked out ones to the warehouse. We heard his footsteps come into the room, and the door opened up. Theo walked in, blood splattered on his shirt, coming from a hole in his shoulder, with the blood dripping down his arm.

"THEO" I screamed as I gasped at the wound.

"Don't worry, princess, It is just a flesh wound. The doctor will come and patch it up soon." Theo said. Taking my hand in his good hand.

"But-" Before I could finish my sentence, he pulled me in and kissed me on the lips.

"Come on, everything has been dealt with. You are safe now." Theo said.

Edna and the maid walked out of the room. He grabbed my hand again, and guided me out of the room. He closed the door and we walked into the living room. We sat on the couch. The doctor came in and started to work on Theo's shoulder. I watched them at a distance.

"You are Ms. Ela, correct?" The doctor said, after bandaging Theo's wound.

"Yes" I said, walking closer to Theo.

"Ok, Make sure he does no extreme physical activity, he keeps that arm in a sling, and doesn't let it get wet. I will take my leave now." The doctor said, leaving.

"Ok, Thank you." I said, as Theo rolled his eyes and leaned back on the couch.

"That old man thinks I can't take care of myself," Theo said.

"He is doing his job and you need to listen to him. You are hurt" I said, sitting beside him again, giving a sad look.

"Don't worry princess. I will be ok. This isn't the first time this has happened." Theo said, which made me even sadder.

"Why are you an undercover spy if you know it could kill you?" I blurted out. Theo gave a shocked expression. Then he smirked.

"I thought you didn't want to know about that part of my life, princess." he said, giving a chuckle.

"It's to protect everything I care about. I also want to protect Liam and Avery. My parents were killed from a malicious attack from a mafia war leader. I made a promise there that I would become an undercover spy and take down the bad mafia leaders." Theo said, staring off into space.

"I'm sorry" I said, looking at the sadness in his eyes.

"Don't be, it was a long time ago. I had to move on. Now I am strong enough to protect the ones I love and care about, even if it gets me hurt." Theo said, tilting my face to his to where we are inches apart.

"It is getting late. Go to bed, and get some rest. I will see you in the morning princess." Theo said, placing a kiss on my forehead then going up the stairs to his room.

I sighed and went up to my room. I got ready for bed, and studied my Bible for a little bit. Then I layed in bed and drifted off to sleep. I still felt bad for Theo, but gave it to God to handle.

24

Memories of the Past

Theo woke up from his nightmare. The memories of his parents 'accident' flooding his mind. He punched his pillow with his good hand. He hated when the memories came back to remind him that he couldn't protect his parents.

He looked at the clock, 3:00 A.M. He didn't want to be up this early, but figured it would be worse to try to go back to sleep and have to think of those memories again. He got out of bed and put shoes on.

He walked to Ela's room and opened her door quietly. He stayed at the door frame and watched her sleep for a little while. Then he closed the door and went down stairs. He dressed in all black so to not be noticed.

He wrote a note and put it on the table. Then he left the house, got in his Bugatti and drove off. He arrived at the graveyard twenty minutes later. He got out of his car and walked to his parents grave.

"Mom, Dad, I am sorry I couldn't protect you. I am sorry I haven't visited you in a while. I know you probably wouldn't be happy with my choices since you've been gone. But I wanted to tell you, that I found someone I truly love. I found my soulmate. She loves me too and has agreed to marry me. I wish I could tell you this in person. I know in the past you wanted me to be with June, but I just can't. I love Ela and I vow to protect her from any harm. I miss you guys. I hope you are doing amazing in heaven. Grandma is doing well. I am taking care of her and the villa. I love you guys." Theo said.

"Theo?" a familiar voice said behind him. He turned around.

"Ela, what are you doing here?" Theo said, shocked.

"I woke up and saw the note on the table, the maid dropped me off to find you and make sure you were ok" Ela said.

"I am fine, just came to see my parents and to talk to them" Theo said, pulling Ela close so she doesn't get cold.

"What were they like?" Ela asked.

"They were the sweetest people you would have ever met. They loved church and God. They tried to help everyone they crossed paths with. They were my role models. They valued family and spending time with God over work. They wanted me to have a family, so they arranged a marriage between June and me. I always thought of June as a sister and nothing more. My parents didn't see it that way though. Well, my dad started gambling, and he gambled against the wrong person. The person staged an 'accident' and killed them." Theo said.

"What happened to that person?" Ela asked.

"When I started training and got a little older, I challenged the person and won back everything that was stolen, then I gave him punishment and handed him over to the police, I gained control of his gang and he was killed in prison." Theo said, hugging Ela from behind with his good hand as they stared at the graves.

"They are probably mad at me for the decisions I have made since they passed." Theo said. Ela turned around and put her hand on his cheek.

"They are in heaven, God had a reason for everything that has happened, I think part of that reason was to make you stronger so you could protect the ones you care about. He knows you will struggle and he is probably telling your parents all the good things you have done for him. I am sure that if your parents saw you now they would be so happy of all the accomplishments you have achieved. They would be proud of you, and happy to know that you are happy. Don't lower yourself so much that it makes you feel bad" Ela said. Theo turned Ela around to face the grave stones again.

"Mom, Dad, This is Ela, the love of my life. My fiance." Theo said, putting his good hand around her waist.

"Nice to meet you Mr. and Mrs. Ambrose. Too bad we couldn't meet in person. Your son is amazing, I hope you are looking down from heaven being proud of him." Ela said, with a smile.

Theo watched her, smiling and happy he made the right choice to have her by his side. Theo's heart swelled every time he watched her do something. He was truly in love with her. He was happy to know she loved him and supported him as well.

"Come on, princess. Let's go back home, before we both catch a cold." Theo said.

"Okay," Ela said.

Theo grabbed her hand and guided back to his car. They got in and he drove back home. The sun was starting to rise. Theo looked over to Ela who was fast asleep in the passenger seat. He smiled and sped up a little.

Theo got out and picked up Ela, bridal style and carried her into the house. He carried her up the stairs and laid her in her bed. He moved the hair out of her face, he put the covers over her and closed the door as he left.

He went downstairs, feeling exhausted with his arm hurting from picking her up. He sat on the couch, in pain. He looked at the wound to make sure it didn't bust open. There was no bleeding so he just took some pain medicine and laid on the couch.

Replaying what Ela told him over in his head. He smiled, feeling happy and intrigued. As long as he met her, he never knew she would comfort him like that. He replayed everything as the medicine started to take effect.

He woke up to Edna gently shaking him. He sat up and looked at the wound. Still no bleeding, but a little hurt. He put the sling back on his arm before Ela woke up. He went upstairs and freshened up.

When he came back downstairs. He saw everyone at the table, he sat down with them. They said the blessing, then ate the breakfast the maid prepared. He then excused himself from the table when he was finished.

He went into the study and got to work. His shoulder still hurt but he needed to get the work done. Ela wouldn't allow it though as she came into the study and took the work away from him.

"The doctor said you need to rest to heal. Why are you working again?" she said,

"Princess, that work has to get done" Theo said.

"Work that your assistant can do. You need to rest" Ela said.

Ela dragged Theo out of the study and made him sit on the couch. Theo obeyed her as he didn't want to make her upset. Ela went into the kitchen, and Theo stayed on the couch. He got his phone out and called his assistant to let him know. Ela came back and handed Theo some of the get well tea. Theo accepted and took a sip. He watched her sit beside him and grab the remote. She put on a Christian movie and they sat there the rest of the afternoon. When it was finally night time, Theo gave Ela a kiss for the night and went to bed, still in pain.

25

Finding Her Purpose

I woke up the next morning, feeling like I was missing something. I got up at 5:00 A.M., did a morning devotional, then got ready for the day. I went down the stairs, and saw that the maid made breakfast, but the other lights were off.

I walked closer to the study and saw the light still on. I went inside, and saw Theo working at his desk, the sling off of his arm. I watched him for a while, my arms folded. I don't think he noticed me in the doorway.

"What do you think you are doing?" I said, which scared him into dropping his pen. He looked up at me with a shocked expression.

"Princess, what are you doing up so early?" he said, giving an awkward chuckle.

"I am always up this early, when I sleep well, I usually just stay in my room till I know everyone else is awake. Why are you working? Why don't you have your sling on?" I said, grabbing the sling of the small side table.

"Heh, umm, I just um" Theo said, nervously.

"I know you have a lot to do, and it is important, but you also need to rest. You are not going to get any better if you don't. Now, please let your assistant do that work and go rest." I said, helping him put the sling on his arm.

"You're not gonna let this go, are you princess?" Theo said.

"Nope, not till I make sure you are healing like you are supposed to" I said, giving him a smirk, as I kissed his cheek.

"Now, come one, out of the study. Let's go watch the sunrise in the garden with some coffee." I said, grabbing his good hand and guiding him out of the study.

We made our way into the kitchen and got some coffee. Then we went outside to the garden and sat on the chairs. We talked while we watched the sunrise. Theo went silent and I knew he was talking to God.

'Heavenly Father, thank you for waking me up and giving me the strength to get ready. Thank you for allowing me to get closer to you and be able to be free. Thank you for helping me all those times. Help Theo to not be so stubborn and to just rest so you can heal him. Keep us safe and protected through this day. I pray I can be the person you would have me to be. Thank you for all of my blessings. I pray for Edna and the maid and Theo. Lord, I don't know why I feel this way, but I feel like I am missing something important in my life. Lord only you know what it is, if it is your will help me to see what that something is. I pray for all the animals I will work with today and in the future. I pray today will be a good day and that you bless everyone I come in contact with. Thank you for this beautiful day. I pray you help us to get to our destinations safely. In your holy and powerful name I pray, Amen.'

I prayed while watching the sunrise and drinking my coffee. I felt the weight being lifted off my shoulders as I gave it to God. The maid then called us in for breakfast. So we went in and sat at the dining room table. We said "good morning" to Edna then blessed the food.

We ate pancakes and fruit. We had a peaceful breakfast. After breakfast, we excuse ourselves from the table. I headed up the stairs and finished getting ready for the day. Then I grabbed my purse and headed back downstairs. I saw Theo at the bottom of the stairs waiting for me.

"Where are you going?" I ask, as I make it to the bottom of the stairs.

"The maid had to take Grandma to some places, so I am gonna take you to work, and spend the day with you, since you won't let me work," Theo said, with a challenging look on his face.

"Okay, but you are just gonna sit on the stool the whole day." I said, giving the same challenging look, and smirking.

"Okay, princess" he said, giving a sigh as we walked out of the house.

We rode to my building listening to contemporary Christian music. We arrived and got out of the car. I unlocked the doors and we went inside. Theo turned the lights on and sat on the stool. I started to begin my work.

I logged into the computer and got the schedules going. I refilled water bowls in the adoption habitats. I fed them their food and made sure the enclosures were clean. I went to the back and did the same things with the rehab enclosures. I then went to check on Brownie in the pasture.

Brownie was going to be adopted next week by a woman who had a ranch. I gave Brownie some hay, and cleaned the dirt off of his body. After that, I went back inside, and saw Theo talking on the phone to someone. I gave him a smile as he hung up.

"Princess, I have a surprise for you this afternoon." Theo said.

"What is it?" I asked.

"It won't be a surprise if I told you," Theo said. I sighed as he chuckled.

"Don't forget, tomorrow, we are going to the court for you to testify," Theo said.

"Okay" I said.

A delivery man came in with the large fish tanks we ordered. We thanked him and I got to work building the tanks. Once they were built I filled them up with water, for the fishes that were supposed to arrive this afternoon, from a fish store going out of business. I went and checked emails. I noticed one that just came in.

'I have a green tree python and a milk snake, I am moving and can't take them with me. Can you take them off of my hands? Thanks.'

I replied back, saying to bring them over. I got the back ready for them to be examined when they show up. Forty minutes later the snakes arrived, I got the papers ready and took them to the back. I got the green tree python out of the container. I gave it the name

Emerald and examined it. Everything was normal and it was doing well. So I put it back into the container and gave it a thawed mouse.

I then got the milk snake, which I named Potter, and examined it. It looked like the tail had been chewed on and is now missing. I examined it then put some medicine on the tail. Once I finished I made the adoption enclosure for Emerald, making sure to include a bunch of branches for it to climb on.

I set up the rehab enclosure for Potter and put both snakes in their enclosures. Then I went back to Theo to see what he was doing. He bought us lunch and spread it out on the back counter. We ate barbecue with fried green tomatoes.

The fish arrived an hour later. We unboxed them and started to organize and acclimate them in tanks by breed. There were two zebra pleco, one blue diamond angelfish, three red coral teacup platy, one snowball pleco, one clown pleco, four super blue emperor kerri tetra, ten neon tetra, two red dragon guppy, three orange sailfin molly, three blue topaz, two double tail betta, and seven goldfish.

Once they were acclimated to the tanks we popped the bags they came in and let them swim in the tank. We gave them some fish food and let them get used to the tanks. Theo took the box and bags to the dumpster.

Two families came in, I took one family and Theo took the other. The family I had wanted a lizard for their son, so I took them to see Cici (leopard gecko) first. They said she was perfect, so I got her out of the cage and put her in a travel cage while they filled out adoption paperwork. I packed the goodies in a bag for them.

They thanked me and took Cici home with them. I put the information from the forms they filled out into the computer. Theo brought Echo (the pit puppy) up to the counter with the family. We got everything set for them while they filled the forms out. They took Echo home with them.

An hour passed, and a customer came in. He asked if we had any spiders. I showed him Stricker (an Amazon blonde tarantula). He agreed to take her so I put her in a travel container and took him to the counter. He filled out the forms while I set up the bag.

The end of the day came and I cleaned up everything. Then we made sure everything was good for the night. Then we closed up the store and went to Theo's car.

"So, you're gonna tell me the surprise now?" I asked with a challenging look.

"Ok, so you know how you say you don't know much about yourself or your family?" Theo said.

"Yeah, what about it?" I asked.

"Ela, I figured out who you are. I found your parents. They live in Mississippi, five hours from here." Theo said, handing me a folder.

"I don't understand, I was told I was an orphan ever since I was born, because my parents died." I said, looking through the folder.

"No, you were kidnapped from your parents when you were born in the hospital. They looked for years for you. They eventually figured you had died. Your last name is Everhart. Your parents want to meet you tomorrow after we get out of court." Theo said, tears started to flow from my eyes.

"This is incredible. Do you think they would accept who I am now?" I asked, as Theo wiped my tears away with his good hand.

"I think they are going to love you" Theo said, starting the car and driving off.

We made it back home. We walked into the dining room and sat at the table with Edna. We blessed the food, then began to eat. We studied our Bibles for a few hours then went to bed. I dreamed of finally meeting my family and being one again.

26

Court and Meeting Ela's Family

Theo woke up, dreading today. He knew after the court session he would have to take Ela to meet her parents. He also knew that she might want to stay with them instead of him.

'Lord, give me strength for today. Lord it is going to be a hard day, not only for her but for me too. Let your will be done. Your plans are always perfect. I need as much strength as you can give me. I pray that if it is your will, that she gets to know her parents, but that she also stays by my side.'

Theo prayed while he was getting ready for the dreadful day. He wanted Ela to be happy, but he didn't know if he could give her up and let her go. He finished getting ready and went down stairs. He saw Edna in the living room.

"Grandma, would it be evil of me to not let her meet her parents and just keep her to myself?" Theo asked, already knowing the answer, but not wanting to listen to himself.

"Theo, you already know the answer to that. God has a plan, trust him. Ela is a good girl, she will make the right decision. She loves you or she wouldn't have forgiven you so many times. She knows God is by her side. Trust her." Edna said, putting her hand on her grandson's arm.

"I know, I just don't know if I can handle losing her, if she decides to stay with them. She would be in a completely different state. She wouldn't be by my side, and I wouldn't get to see her every-day." Theo said, sitting on the couch, sad.

Theo put his hand through his hazel hair. He wondered if he could get away with keeping her. He knew God wouldn't be happy with any of the plans he was thinking. He got his Bible and started to read.

"Listen, God has got this. He knows what is right and what you both need. Trust that whatever he has planned, it is the right plan." Edna said, as she started to walk out of the living room.

Theo sighed and put his Bible down. He heard Ela come out of her room. He looked up the stairs and saw how beautiful she was. He knew he had to give it all to God including her. He cleared his throat and held out his hand to her. He was determined that he would spend the rest of this day with her, as if it was their last day together.

"Are you ready for today, princess?" Theo said.

"I think I am, I know I have you and God by my side" Ela said, Theo gave a small smile.

They made their way to Theo's Bugatti. He helped her in and got in on the driver's side. They made it to the courthouse twenty five minutes later. They parked and went inside. The sheriff guided them to a seat and told them to wait to be called up.

Theo watched as they went through the trial, then they called Ela up. He gave her hand a squeeze of comfort and watched her as she went up and told the truth. After she testified, they sentenced Vincent and his friends to life in prison. The gavel went down and the trial was over.

"You did so good, I am so proud of you for being brave." Theo said, as Ela came to his side.

"Thanks, I just looked towards you every time I felt uncomfortable. If it wasn't for you and God I wouldn't be able to do it." Ela said, clinging to Theo's arm.

They left the courthouse and got in Theo's car. Theo started the long drive to Mississippi. He knew the closer they got, the possibility grew for Ela to stay and leave his side. He kept calm and kept talking to God. He knew there would be no choice but to let her go if she decides to stay with them.

They arrived at her parents house four hours later. They got out of the vehicle and made their way to the front door. Theo knocked with his good hand. An older man opened the door.

"Please, come in, come in" The man said.

"Are you really our Ela?" an older woman asked.

"Ma'am This is the report and DNA test. She is in fact your daughter. My name is Theo, I saved her from her kidnapper." Theo said, handing the folder to the woman.

"Ohhh" The woman said, looking at the contents of the folder and tearing up.

"Ela, this is your mom, Renona Everhart, and your dad John Everhart." Theo said.

"Our daughter is finally home!" Renona said, tears flowing.

They shared a hug with Ela. They stayed in that moment for a while. Theo watched Ela, as she had tears of joy and comfort. They broke their hug and dragged Ela to their couch. Theo stayed in the entrance of the living room. They showed Ela a bunch of photos and books. Theo kept thinking he is losing the love of his life, right there in front of his eyes.

'God, you have to give me strength. I can't bear to see her leave me. I want her to be happy, but this hurts, Lord. What is your plan? Please help me, heavenly father'

Theo kept praying, begging God to not make Ela leave his side. Theo felt tears come to his eyes so he went outside. He got his phone out and dialed Liam. Liam picked up after the third ring.

"Hey man, I need your help, I am in Mississippi with Ela, meeting her parents. I am having evil thoughts of kidnapping her away from them. I want her to be happy, but I can't imagine living without her." Theo said.

"Theo, man, you got to trust God more. I believe Ela will make the right decision. When you are having those evil thoughts go to God, and read the Bible. I got to go, Avery isn't feeling well and Bella Rose is crying. I will talk to you later, bye man." Liam said, hanging up.

Theo sighed and put his phone away. He knew Liam was right, so he talked to God once more, then went back inside. He saw Ela and her parents laughing. His heart clenched seeing her happy.

"Ela, can you come here for a second?" Theo said.

"Sure," she said.

"We will be right back Mr. and Mrs. Everhart." Theo said, taking Ela hand and guiding her outside.

"Ela, I know you are incredibly happy and I don't want to ruin that happiness. I need to know, Do you plan to stay here with them?" Theo said.

"Oh umm, I don't know, I haven't thought about that. Wait, if I choose to stay with them, what does that mean for us?" Ela asked, a sad look on her face

"Well if you choose to stay, I will let you stay here and I will go back home. We can stay engaged only if you want to, if you do choose to stay. This is your decision. Either way I still love your princess" Theo said.

"This is a hard decision to make. I love you Theo, but I also now know I have parents. I haven't seen them for twenty one years. I never got a chance to even know them." Ela said, trying to think.

"Whatever you choose, I support you. Whenever you want to come back home, I will come get you, you will be by my side, no matter how many hours we are apart. If you do choose to stay, I completely understand. I know how it feels to want to be close to your parents" Theo said, holding her hands.

"Theo, I … I want to stay. At least for a few months. I want to get to know them more, and be able to be a part of their lives. I will continue to be your fiance and we will still get married in eight months." Ela said, a guilty expression on her face.

"Don't feel bad princess, I understand. Anytime you want to come back home, just give me a call. I love you, princess. I am gonna go, before it gets dark. I will have someone come deliver some of your stuff over here. Edna packed you a travel bag, you can use until the rest of your stuff arrives. Remember I am only one call away. I love you princess" Theo said, placing a kiss on her forehead, then kissing her lips.

"Bye princess" Theo said, letting go of her hands and walking to his car.

They waved goodbye to each other and Theo began to drive away. He started to tear up, not only did he lose his parents, but also his partner and his love. He prayed to God again.

'Lord, I really don't know what your plan is. I need you, she is the one you have for me, I know it. How am I supposed to keep going knowing she is so far away. How am I supposed to feel knowing she won't be at the house everytime I come home? What is your plan?'

Theo felt hopeless, and alone. He knew God was with him and that he wasn't actually alone, but he always had Ela by his side, since he bought her. He finally gave it to God and headed home.

He arrived at home and went inside. Edna was in the living room crocheting a blanket. He went into the living room and sat beside her. He felt sad, he had to let Ela go.

"She decided to stay with her parents, didn't she?" Edna said.

"Yep, she wanted to be a part of their lives and she wanted to spend some time with them. I let her do it, I let her go" Theo said, with a sigh.

"Oh, Theo. It is gonna be ok. God has a plan. Do you remember when your parents died when you were younger? You were so upset, that you wanted to kill yourself just to be with them. You couldn't handle being apart from them. Think of how she feels. She just found out her parents are alive, and she isn't an orphan. Think of all of those years she missed because she was kidnapped and told she was an orphan. It is understandable she would want to be around them at the moment. And just think, You are still engaged and will have a wedding in eight months, right?" Edna said, putting the blanket down and holding his hand.

"Yeah, you're right. Thanks Grandma" Theo said.

"You're welcome. Now go eat your dinner then go upstairs and rest." Edna said, going back to the blanket.

27

Avery and Liam's POV

"Bella rose, calm down, you are ok, love." Liam said, with the baby crying in his arms.

Avery and Liam got out of the hospital yesterday, all was calm the first night. Then this morning Avery wasn't feeling good, with a fever and a migraine. Bella Rose started crying after being fed at 4:00 A.M. this morning.

"Liam, just hand her here, she is probably just tired. I am okay enough to get her to sleep" Avery said, exhausted.

"Ok, but as soon as she falls asleep she goes to the bassinet and you are getting rest." Liam said, handing Bella over to Avery.

Avery took her and started to sing a lullaby while rocking her. After thirty minutes, Bella calmed down and went to sleep. With a sigh of relief, Avery put Bella in the bassinet beside her. Liam sighed and went out of their room.

Liam came back thirty minutes later with some water and soup. He placed the tray on the nightstand beside Avery. He sat beside her on the bed.

"You need to get something in you. I know you don't have an appetite, but with you breastfeeding Bella, you need to keep your strength up. Please eat, my love." Liam said.

Avery nodded and took the tray, she forced herself to eat the soup and drink the water. After she was done, she handed the tray to Liam and laid back down. He put the tray on the nightstand and checked her temperature.

"One hundred degrees, at least it went down some. I still can't believe the hospital let you go home, knowing you had gotten an infection." Liam said.

"Babe, it is fine. I am taking the antibiotics they gave me. I am stronger than you think. I wonder how Ela is doing with her parents?" Avery said.

"I heard from Theo. She decided to stay with her parents for a little while, but they are still engaged and will have the wedding in eight months. Theo says they are doing great together. He left her with them, they will take care of her. Now please get some rest." Liam said, kissing her forehead.

Liam walked out of the room with the bassinet. He stayed in the living room watching Bella Rose in the bassinet. He got his Bible and started reading and spending time with God. An hour passed, Bella Rose woke up hungry.

Liam went to the freezer and unthawed the breast milk Avery pumped before. He put it in a bottle and went to Bella. He gave her the bottle and she was satisfied. He held her in his arms, feeling blessed to have her.

He burped her, then changed her diaper and she went back to sleep. Liam put her back in the bassinet. He went to check on Avery, she was still sleeping. He closed the door and went back down to Bella.

Liam turned the TV down on low and watched the football game. Bella was used to sleeping through loud noises. Avery slept for two hours and came out of the room and into the living room. She sat beside Liam on the couch. Liam checked her temperature again.

"Ninety-nine degrees, that is better than it was. Are you feeling any better?" Liam asked.

"Yeah, the migraine is gone." Avery said, leaning her head on his shoulder.

"Can you believe God blessed us with this little miracle?" Liam said, watching Bella in the bassinet. They both smiled and thanked God again for giving them Bella.

28

Going Home

I woke up in the guest bedroom of my parents house. It has been seven months since Theo and my parents let me stay here. Theo and I kept in touch through our phones, but I still missed him.

I got ready and went into the kitchen. My dad was there making coffee. I sat at the table with my Bible and journal and morning devotional. My dad handed me a cup of coffee.

"Sweetheart, we love that you are with us again. We also know you have a fiance and probably miss him. You seem sad lately." my dad said.

"Yeah, I miss him. Even though we talk on the phone, I still miss being by his side. I also miss working at the center with the animals." I said, sipping the coffee.

"Why don't we head over there and you can give us a tour of your building and the animals." My dad said.

"Are you sure? That is a four hour drive. Do you really want to go all the way over there?" I asked, a little excited.

"Let's do it, plus it will be fun to see all that you have accomplished." My dad said, as my mom came into the kitchen.

"Ok" I said, Feeling happier.

We got ready and left the house thirty minutes later. I guided my dad to the building. We arrived and went inside. Assistant Scott was working the counter. I greeted him and showed my parents all of the animals.

"These are incredible, I am so proud of you sweetheart." My mom said,

"Thanks Mom" I said, still feeling weird being able to call someone mom.

An hour passed, and we were playing with the animals when someone came in. I looked at the door, it was … Theo. My heart raced being able to see him in person again. He talked to Assistant Scott, then looked around. His eyes landed on me and we stood frozen for a moment.

"Ela?" Theo said, shocked.

"Yeah" I said, nodding.

"ELA! Princess!" Theo said, running towards me and picking me up and spinning.

"I missed you" Theo said, as I giggled.

"I missed you too," I said.

He sat me back down, excitement showing on his face. My parents greeted him and he did the same to them. He held my hand as he spoke to them. His arm completely healed.

"Is this what you meant to come to Ela's building?" Theo asked my dad.

"Yep, our daughter has been sad the past two weeks. We knew she needed to be by your side again, since you are the one who saved her and brought her back to us. I figured you both can benefit from seeing each other in person." my dad said, as we looked at each other and smiled.

"You only have one month before the wedding, so we figured it was time for you to come back to the place you first felt safe and be with the person who helped you feel safe and helped you grow." my mom said,

"You hurt my daughter, I won't hesitate to come after you though." My dad said.

"Don't worry sir, I will protect her with my life." Theo said, smiling at me.

We waved goodbye to my parents and Theo led me to his car. He opened the door for me and helped me in. He got in on the driver's side.

"Where are we going?" I said, as he started to drive.

"I am taking you to our park, with Avery, Liam, and the seventh month old baby, Bella." Theo said.

We arrived at the park and got out of the car. We went to the entrance of the park and walked in. We saw Avery and Liam walking with a stroller. We walked over to them.

"Hey guys" I said, as they looked shocked when they looked at me.

"Ela!" Avery screamed and hugged me.

"Hey Avery," I said, giggling. She guided me to Bella.

"Aww, Look at you, you have grown" I said, as Avery handed her to me.

"Have you guys gone back to work yet?" I asked, as I held Bella.

"Yeah, Avery's mom watches Bella While we work," Liam said.

We walked through the park. enjoying spending time with each other. Theo was picking on Liam for not being able to calm Bella in the beginning. Avery and I smiled as we continued to walk. We stopped at a little cafe and went in.

"What do you want, Princess?" Theo asked, as Avery and Liam smirked.

"Hot chocolate and a blueberry muffin." I said, paying them no mind.

We all ordered the stuff we wanted and sat at a table. We blessed the food we got and began to eat. Then both Liam and Avery smirked again.

"When do you two lovebirds plan to get married?" Liam said, elbowing Theo. Theo pushed his arm away.

"Next month, you know this, You are the best man and she is the maid of honor for Ela" Theo said, pointing to Avery.

"Come on Theo, you know he is messing with you" Avery said, picking up the baby from the stroller.

"Yeah, yeah" Theo said, drinking his coffee.

We stayed in the little cafe, Liam and Theo kept talking. Avery and I played with Bella, who was just a happy baby. We stayed for three hours, then left the cafe. We waved Avery and Liam and Bella goodbye and walked back to the cherry blossom tree. Theo played music on his phone and offered his hand out to me.

"Would you like to dance, princess?" Theo said.

"Let's do it," I said.

We danced to the music until the sun went down. Then we went to Theo's car and got in. We made it back to the house and went inside. I walked in, Edna and the maid looked shocked to see me. Edna came and hugged me.

"Oh, dear, I am so glad you are back. We all missed you." Edna said.

"I missed you guys too," I said, hugging them back.

Theo stood behind me, smiling. He grabbed my hand and led me further inside the house. We stopped at the bottom of the stairs. He kissed my forehead.

"Go get some rest princess, you will have plenty of time to chit chat tomorrow, good night" Theo said.

"Okay, good night." I said, as I made my way up the stairs and back into my room. I got ready for bed and went to sleep, feeling at peace for being home.

29

Helping the Two Heroes

Theo woke up and got ready in his spy outfit. He went downstairs and met with Edna and Ela. He gave Ela a kiss on the forehead. He also hugged Edna.

"Where are you going so early?" Ela asked, as she sat at the table.

"I am gonna go help Avery and Liam on a hard case they are working on. I will be back sometime later tonight. If you need to go anywhere, ask Assistant Scott. I love you princess, enjoy your day." Theo said, giving her a hug.

"Okay, be safe," Ela said.

Theo walked out of the house and got in his Bugatti. He drove to the police station where he was meeting Avery and Liam. He arrived and went inside, he said hi to the secretary and sheriff. He walked into Avery's office.

"Okay, we are going after a mafia boss named Angelo. He started gaining a reputation a year after we caught Jace for good. He is quickly starting to become one of the most feared mafia bosses this year. His gang is called the demon snakes. We don't have much information on him as he usually hides in the shadows. He also has police from another state working with him, so we need to watch our backs as he will try to get cops to turn on eachother. Theo, we know he is going to be at the mafia hang out today, to introduce his daughter at the party. We need you to go as Theodore, with your gang and get as much information as you can." Avery said.

"I am going to pose as one of your gang members to help you."
Liam said.

"Okay, let's do this, we will keep you updated." Theo said.

Liam got dressed in a spy outfit and Theo called up some of
his gang members. Theo knew most gangs knew about him, he also
knew those same gangs feared him. Theo put his mask and jacket on.

They exited the police station and headed to Theo's Bugatti.
They made their way to Theo's hideout. They got on motorcycles
and headed to the mafia party. They headed inside, the tension in
the air, as other gangs knew who Theodore and the ice dragons were.

Theodore and the gang walked in further. Angelo saw them, and
with a smirk went towards Theodore. Theodore stood, surrounded
by his gang, watching every move Angelo made.

"Theodore of the Ice Dragon gang. What's up?" Angelo said,
stopping in front of Theodore.

"Meh, same old same old, kidnapping people, tormenting people. The usual" Theodore said, being cautious of Angelo, knowing
his tricks.

"I am glad you are here to celebrate my daughter trying to find
a fiance," Angelo said.

"I am not here for her, I already have my mafia queen. I just
came because of the invitation, to show you 'respect'" Theodore said.

"Oh, well, either way you are here, let me introduce you to her."
Angelo said, with an evil smirk.

"Whatever" Theodore said.

They walked to where Angelo's daughter was. Angelo introduced her to Theo and the gang. Theo didn't care, he was just trying
to keep an eye on Angelo.

"Like I said, I already found my queen, but you are free to
choose one of my single gang members, if you would like," Theodore
said, with a snap of his fingers.

The single members of the gang lined up beside Theo. Theo
came up with a plan, if one of his members gets chosen by Angelo's
daughter, then that member can get all the information they need.
Liam watched Theo put the plan into action.

"Dad, I want this one, he is so handsome, please Daddy" Angelo's daughter begged her father.

"What do you say Theodore, do you allow one of your members to marry my daughter" Angelo said, a wry smile on his face.

"Sure, why not." Theodore said, nodding to the gang member she chose.

The gang member nodded to Theodore, and walked to the side of Angelo's daughter. Angelo's daughter clung to the gang member's arm. Angelo then guided them to the stage.

"I want to thank each and everyone of you for coming for my daughter. She has chosen her husband, here is Danielle and her future husband from the Ice Dragon gang, Simon. With the marriage of these two, our two gangs will be united. So I want to ask the leader of the Ice Dragon gang, Theodore, to come up and say a few words" Angelo said, gesturing towards Theodore.

"Thank you, Angelo. Congrats to the happy couple, hope you treat each other well. May everything go according to plan and our gangs work together. Simon, make sure to make her happy." Theodore said, walking off the stage.

The party went on, as everyone talked and drank wine. Theo kept watching Angelo's movements as he was surrounded by his gang. Simon stuck to the plan and took Angelo's daughter to a private room, to see if they could get more information.

They came back an hour later. Simon nodded to Theodore to say the plan was successful. Theodore nodded as well. They stayed at the party for two more hours.

"Angelo, thank you for inviting us to this party. We got to go now" Theodore said to Angelo.

"Alright, leave Simon to our care, we will take care of him" Angelo said, as Theodore nodded.

Theodore and the gang left the party. They went towards their motorcycles. Theo turned towards the rest of the gang.

"Did you get the recorder from simon?" Theo asked his gang members.

"We got it" one of the members held it in their hands.

"Good, give it to Liam to take back to the station. Once everyone leaves the party we will ambush Angelo and take him in" Theodore said.

The gang member handed Liam the recorder. Liam got on his motorcycle and headed for the station. The gang members moved all of their motorcycles away from the party so as to not be spotted.

They waited for Avery and Liam to show up. When they did, they waited for the right moment. Then Avery and the police, with the gang as backup, ambushed Angelo and took him into custody.

The sun had gone down hours ago. Theo took the claim of Angelo's gang. Simon kept Danielle safe, and with him. Avery, Liam, and Theo went into Angelo's warehouse and took everything they could find as evidence.

"Thank you, Danielle, for helping bring your father into custody" Theodore said.

"No problem. He always wanted to control every aspect of my life. At least now, I have freedom." she said,

"To protect you, you will be a part of the gang, and only if you want to, you can stay with Simon, it seems like he has taken a liking to you." Theo said, looking over at Simon watching them.

"Thank you, Theodore" she said, then walked to Simon's side. Simon helped her on the motorcycle and took off.

"Good job all of you. Go home and rest. I will give you updates on the next mission, when the time comes. Good night everyone" Theodore said, getting on his motorcycle.

Theo headed back to the warehouse. He got in his Bugatti and headed home. It was 11:00 P.M. Whenever he arrived home. He walked in, fixed him a snack and went into the living room.

He noticed Ela asleep on the couch. He smiled and pushed her hair out of her face. He kneeled beside her, and placed a kiss on her cheek and forehead.

"Princess, wake up" Theo said, placing his hand on her shoulder.

He chuckled and picked her up bridal style and took her to her bed. He put her under the covers and left her room. He closed the door behind him. He went back down to the living room. He sat on the couch and ate his snack, while playing on his phone. He then got ready for bed and went to sleep.

30

The Wedding and Honeymoon

I woke up the morning of the wedding. The month went by like normal and it was finally the day of the wedding. Me, my mom, and Avery were getting ready at a hotel. I put on my wedding dress that had pink faded at the bottom of it.

Avery and my mom were wearing purple bridesmaid dresses. The bouquet was made with tulips and orchids. My mom put the veil on my curly strawberry blonde hair. The veil was connected to a tiara.

I put the white sparkly heels on. We waited for a little bit. We then arrived at the church and slipped into a room, without Theo or anyone seeing us. There was a knock at the door, My mom opened the door slightly. Edna came in with a small box.

"Here you go dear. Here is your wedding gift from Theo. He already received his. Go ahead and open it." Edna said, handing me the box.

I opened the box and saw a bracelet in the box. I got it out and put it on. It was gorgeous and matched the dress perfectly. My nails were painted a sparkly silver color. Then we were told to get ready as it is about to start.

They exited the room and got into their positions. The music started to play as my dad came into the room. He smiled at me as I stood up.

"You look beautiful sweetheart. He will be so happy to see you." my dad said, holding his hand out to me.

It was time to walk down the aisle. My dad stayed to the side, for the first look. The doors opened revealing me. Theo started to tear up, as my dad came to my side to walk me down the aisle. We arrived at the altar and my dad handed me over to Theo. Theo took my hand and helped me up the stairs. The preacher said a prayer over us before we got started.

"Ladies and gentlemen, we are gathered here today to celebrate the union of Theo Ambrose and Ela Everhart. Theo, please start with your vows." The preacher said.

"Ela, ever since I met you, I had no idea what God had planned. I am so blessed that he put you in my life. I remember the first time I started to love you. I thank God everyday that he allowed me to marry you. I will continue to love you, till the day I die. With this ring I make my commitment to you, to love and cherish you through sickness and troubles. Till death do us part" Theo said, putting the rings on my finger.

"Ms. Ela, it is time for your vows now," the preacher said.

"Theo, I am so glad God had a plan for me and you. If it wasn't for you I probably wouldn't even be alive today. I wouldn't have been able to meet my parents or the friends I have now. I am truly blessed by God to be able to be by your side, not only as a friend but also as your wife. With this ring, I promise to love and cherish you. I vow to be the Proverb 31 wife I am meant to be. Through sickness and troubles that come our way. Till death do us part" I said, putting the wedding band on Theo's finger.

"Theo, You may now kiss your bride" The preacher said, backing away.

Theo wrapped his hand around my waist and pulled me close. We kissed as people cheered and applauded. Avery handed my bouquet back to me. I threw the bouquet behind me and Danielle caught it. We all clapped, as Theo pulled me closer to his side and smiled at me.

We walked down the aisle and had our first dance. Everyone was stunned by our slow dance. We laughed and had fun as we danced. Then the father daughter dance came. My dad took my hand and we danced as everyone watched. Theo danced with Edna. Then everyone came and danced. We all danced for a while.

We cut our cake an hour later. Then everyone started doing their speeches. It was a magical day. Everyone enjoyed the day. We took pictures and played games. Everyone started to leave and we thanked them for coming.

"Alright, lovebirds, it is time you go on your honeymoon" Liam said, holding Bella.

"Yep, we are going. Let's go. We will be back in a week, Grandma" Theo said, taking my hand and guiding me away from the outside of the church.

We got in the car and drove to the airport. Theo wouldn't tell me where we were going. We arrived at the airport and boarded the private jet. We flew for about fourteen hours. When we landed, I was kind of confused.

"Where are we?" I asked Theo.

"Japan" Theo said, with a smirk, grabbing our stuff.

"I noticed you looking at images of Japan last month. So I made it to where we can take our honeymoon to Japan." he said, grabbing my hand.

We got out of the jet and went inside a beautiful house. Theo put the stuff down and turned the lights on. I looked around the house.

"Whose house are we in?" I asked.

"Ours," Theo said.

"What?" I asked, a shocked look on my face.

"I bought the house for us. We can come whenever we want to. My queen" Theo said, grabbing my waist and pulling me close.

"Oh, so I am not your princess anymore?" I asked, a challenging look on my face.

"You are my princess and my queen. We are married now after all" Theo said, also giving a challenging look.

"Come on, let's go explore." Theo said, after placing a kiss on my forehead.

I followed him out and we started to explore what Tokyo, Japan had to offer. We started to check out all of the shops and gardens. We had fun, doing new experiences and laughing together. I also didn't know Theo could speak Japanese.

"Kon'nichiwa, kankōkyaku ni iku no ni saitekina basho wa dokodesu ka" Theo asked a local person.

"Mukojima Hyakkaen teien" The man said, pointing in a direction.

"What did you ask him?" I inquired.

"Good afternoon, what is the best place to go to for tourists? Is what I said" Theo said.

"He recommended a garden?" I asked.

"Yep" Theo said, taking my hand and guiding me to the garden.

I took pictures of all of the flowers and scenery. It was beautiful here. We enjoyed our time on our honeymoon. We felt blessed by God in every way.

31

Back Home

Theo and Ela were exhausted getting off of the private jet. The week went by smoothly. Assistant Scott came to pick them up from the airport. He drove them home. They got out of the vehicle with their suitcases. Edna and the maid threw a welcome back party for Theo and Ela.

"WELCOME HOME!" They screamed, while popping a party popper.

"Awww, thank you Edna," Ela said, grabbing Edna's outstretched hands.

"No, no, I am your Grandma now. You are officially part of the family now. No more being formal" Edna said.

"Thanks, Grandma, but we are pretty exhausted, as it is 7:00 P.M and we have been flying for about fourteen hours. So we are gonna head to bed, and we can celebrate like crazy tomorrow, okay?" Theo said. Edna agreed.

Theo and Ela went up to their room and unpacked their bags. They got ready for bed and did their Bible study and talked with God. They then got in bed and went to sleep. It only took about five minutes to fall asleep as they were completely exhausted

Theo woke up the next morning with Ela laying on his chest. He smiled and brushed his fingers through her hair. She woke up and smiled up at him. They got up and did their morning devotionals. They then got ready and went down for breakfast.

"How was your first night back at your own home?" Edna asked.

"Well, it was a peaceful sleep, I wasn't constantly hearing horns and traffic go by." Theo said. Ela nodded and kept eating.

"So, when are you two going to give me a great grandchild?" Edna said, smiling.

"Grandma, we just got married a week ago. That is a little too early." Ela said.

"Nonsense, I got pregnant with Theo's father a month after I got married." Edna said, Theo and Ela both blushing.

They all finished their breakfast and finished getting ready for church. They headed out the door thirty minutes later. They arrived at church and met Avery and Liam, and Bella in the parking lot. They went inside the church and got ready for worship and the sermon.

Theo held Ela's hand the entire time. The sermon was on boldness and faith. Ela highlighted the verses in her Bible. The sermon finished at twelve and everyone left. Theo, Ela, and Edna went to go eat with Avery and Liam.

They went to a steakhouse to eat. Avery and Ela ordered ribeyes, while Theo and Liam ordered sirloins. Edna ordered fish. They blessed their food and began to eat. Bella started to cry.

"Shhhhh, Bella it's ok, You have already been fed. Let's see if you need a diaper change." Liam said, checking her diaper.

"Here, give her here, I will change her." Avery said.

Liam handed Bella to Avery. Avery took her to the restroom. She came back five minutes later with a happy Bella. She handed Bella to Ela, who gladly took her. Bella giggled in Ela's arms. Theo kept making funny faces at her, which made her giggle even more.

The rest of the day went by smoothly. Theo and Ela went home after night service. They ate supper and got ready for bed. They stayed up till ten to watch a Christian movie, then went to bed and slept peacefully.

32

Surprise

Three weeks went by, and I woke up feeling nauseous. I got out of bed and rushed to the bathroom. Theo came to the door five minutes later. He knocked on the bathroom door.

"Princess, are you okay?" He asked.

"I am fine, I just feel nauseous." I said.

"Open the door" Theo said, I got up and unlocked the door.

Theo came into the bathroom and hugged me. He rubbed my back. I stayed in the hug. We prayed that God would heal the nausea. We went back to bed and tried to go back to sleep as it was 3:00 A.M. I just layed there, as I couldn't sleep. Eventually, I just got out of bed again.

"Still not feeling better?" Theo asked, sitting up in bed.

"Not really," I said.

"I will take you to the doctor when they open in three hours," Theo said, getting out of bed.

We made our way downstairs and sat on the couch. I got my morning devotional and started to read. Liam was making coffee in the kitchen. He came and sat beside me on the couch.

We waited two hours, then got ready to go to the doctor. We headed to the doctors fifteen minutes later. It was a thirty minute trip. We arrived and Theo helped me out. We walked in and Theo filled out the check in paperwork. They took several tests and we waited for an hour. Then a nurse came into the room.

"Congratulations, Mr. and Mrs Ambrose" the nurse said, Theo and I looked confused.

"Oh, right. You are pregnant." the nurse said, walking out. Theo was Excited but I was scared.

"What's wrong?" Theo said, standing in front of me, wiping the tears off my cheeks.

"What if I am not a good mom. What if something bad happens and I lose this baby like in the past." I said, looking at him with tear filled eyes.

"Nothing is going to happen. God will protect this baby. You do a fabulous job whenever you help Avery out with Bella. Trust in God, he will help you. Plus I am now going to be a father. I am so happy" Theo said, hugging me, I smiled as the nurse came back in.

"We have the ultrasound machine ready, if you want to see how far you are measuring." The nurse said.

"Yes please," Theo said.

They guided us to the ultrasound room. The nurse told me to lay on the bed and she started to use the machine. She showed us the little fetus.

"Okay, looks like you are measuring about four weeks along. Here are some papers to help you on your pregnancy journey. Have a good day." the nurse said, handing Theo the papers and showing us out.

I looked at the sonogram pictures, in shock. Theo noticed me and put one of his hands on mine, while driving with the other. I looked up at him, as he smiled at me then turned his attention back towards the road. We arrived home and went inside.

"Where have you two been, we were worried sick about you two." Edna said, coming towards us.

"Sorry, Grandma, I took Ela to the doctor as she was nauseous." Theo said, as Edna gasped.

"Ela dear, are you pregnant?" Edna said, with a hopeful expression.

"Yes" I said, looking down, Theo handed her the sonogram pictures.

"Measuring four weeks," Theo said.

"Oh, thank you Jesus for answering prayers." Edna said, excited.

"Wait, Grandma, you prayed for her to get pregnant so soon." Theo asked.

"Well of course I did, I am not getting any younger, and I want to see my great grandchild" Edna said.

We smiled at each other, knowing Grandma's mischievous ways. I hid my blush with my hands, as Theo pulled me closer to his side. He chuckled at Grandma who was showing the maid the sonogram pictures. Theo guided me to the couch. We sat down, while Theo made a phone call.

"Liam and Avery are coming over with Bella." Theo said, getting off the phone.

"Ok" I said.

We waited for them while reading books. Edna was still so excited, but was taking care of me by giving me tea to help with the nausea. The doorbell rang twenty minutes later. The maid let Avery and Liam in. Avery came and sat beside me hugging me.

"Congrats," Avery said, excited.

"Better start thinking of baby names, dude" Liam said, elbowing Theo, while holding Bella.

"So that will mean, Bella will be a year and five months old whenever you have your baby. oh, this is great, they can grow up together and be friends." Avery said, even more excited. We all laughed at her excitedness.

We spent most of the day playing games and enjoying our little Christian community. Theo then got a call on his phone, so he excused himself from the room and answered. He came back fifteen minutes later in his spy outfit.

"I have to go Princess, I will be back tonight. Have fun with Avery and Liam." Theo said, placing a kiss on my forehead.

"Ok" I said, watching him leave.

Avery and Liam stayed and played for four hours. Then Liam got a call and went to answer it. He came back looking panicked and whispered something to Avery. Her face went pale.

"What's wrong?" I asked, getting worried.

"Theo and his gang lost the fight, he is in the hospital right now. But he is a fighter, please don't worry" Liam said, sighing.

"What! We have to go to him!" I said, getting up from the couch.

Everyone grabbed their stuff and headed to Liam's car. We got in and I kept praying as Liam sped to the hospital. What is going to happen now? We arrived at the hospital some time later.

33

Losing the Status and Gang

Theo woke up in a hospital bed, right as Liam, Avery, ELa and Bella came into the room.

They all gave him sad and sympathetic looks. Ela rushed to his side and sat in a chair beside his bed.

"What happened?" Liam asked.

"We were gonna take down a gang selling illegal drugs in a warehouse. They had an ambush planned, they took everything including the gang members. I managed to escape, but was badly injured. I passed out on a busy street, someone must have called 911" Theo said, sighing and running his hand through his hair.

"You are so blessed by God, that you weren't killed in that moment. How many members did you bring with you?" Liam said.

"All of them, and it still wasn't enough," Theo said.

"I lost the Ice Dragon gang for good. My status and leadership was ripped out from under me." Theo said.

"You should be thanking God that you are still alive, then worrying about losing your gang. God has got a plan, you have to trust him. I am gonna go speak with the doctor and sheriff" Liam said, walking out of the room.

"I am sorry I worried you Princess" Theo said, noticing the worried look on Ela's face.

"It's fine, I am just glad God protected you and you weren't killed" Ela said.

"Your main focus is getting healed, and spending more time with your wife and God" Avery said, trying to calm Bella down.

"You're right, I have a long conversation to have with God" Theo said, nodding.

"Come on Ela, let's go, Let him have some time with God, They have a lot to talk about" Avery said.

"Ok" Ela said, letting go of Theo's hand.

Theo watched as they left the room. He sighed and ran his hand through his hair again. He then looked outside the window and began to talk to God out loud.

"Lord, forgive me for not talking to you sooner. I confess every sin I knowingly and unknowingly committed. You know how I see the members of that gang as family. I want to thank you for helping me escape alive. I don't know what your plan is, Lord, but I trust you. I pray that the members are safe and alive if it is your will. I am so grateful you kept me alive to where I can be there for Ela and our child. Heavenly father, give me the strength I need, to be the husband and father I need to be. Help me to lead my family closer to you. I want to be able to keep them safe, but can't do that without your help, Lord. I can't live my life without you. Lord, give me your strength if it is your will. I need help, Lord. I give it all to you Lord"

Theo talked to God for a little while. A knock on the door sounded, the doctor came in with Liam, Avery, and Ela. Everyone sat down and looked between the doctor and Theo.

"Mr. Ambrose, you are lucky to be alive. You have several broken ribs, a fractured leg, and a concussion. You will have to stay in the hospital for a few days." The doctor said, then left the room.

"God blessed you with your life, man," Liam said, holding Bella.

Ela texted Edna about what happened and what the plan was. Theo and Liam were talking. Theo noticed Ela's worry, he gave a charming smile and went back to talking. Liam and Avery stayed till visiting hours were over. Ela pulled up her chair closer to Theo.

"I love you princess," Theo said, holding her hand.

"I love you too, but you were crazy, you could have gotten killed. What would happen if you got killed and left me and our child?" Ela said.

"I know, I am sorry. Won't be any more mafia missions, I lost the gang" Theo said.

"God probably did that because he has bigger plans for you" Ela said.

"Probably, I still thought of them as family though" Theo said.

"God has a plan, trust him." Ela said, as a nurse brought food in.

"Thank you," Ela said, grabbing the trays.

The hospital food was pretty good. The trays included grilled chicken, baked chips, and chocolate pudding. They also brought tea for drinks. Theo and Ela blessed their food and ate it all. They knew not to take food for granted, as most people in the world barely even got that.

Ela started to make a comfortable spot on the couch beside his bed. The nurse gave Ela a blanket and pillow. Theo watched her, as she was getting everything ready. They talked for a while until they both fell asleep.

Theo woke up the next morning, feeling the pain of what happened the day before. He looked over to where Ela was sleeping. He smiled as she was sleeping peacefully with her hands protecting her stomach. He started to talk to God again.

'God, you know my heart. Give me strength to deal with this pain, Lord. I want to thank you for giving me a loving and caring wife, and for giving us a child together. Let your will be done in our lives. Whatever your plan is for us, I trust you no matter what. Thank you Lord'

Ela woke up ten minutes later. She looked at Theo and they smiled at each other. The nurse came in with some breakfast trays and handed them the trays. Theo blessed the food and they began to eat the bacon, eggs, and biscuit. They finished and Ela got her phone and they began to do a morning devotional, then they worshiped God with some worship music.

Edna came into the room a little later, she brought all of their stuff to them. Edna prayed for healing over Theo. Theo looked at Ela, as she was rubbing her belly. He knew she was scared for the baby, but she couldn't hide the joy in her eyes.

"Princess?" Theo said.

"Yes?" Ela said, looking up.

"God's got this, Everything will go according to his plan." Theo said, giving a reassuring look.

"I know," Ela said. Confusion on her face.

"Let go of the past, and trust in Him," Theo said. That broke Ela, she started to cry.

"Come here" Theo said, patting beside him on the bed. She came over and sat on the bed beside him.

"It's gonna be ok. Everything is going to be wonderful. It wasn't your fault what happened" Theo said, wiping her tears and hugging her gently.

He knew he could always bear the pain for her. No matter how bad he hurt, he would always be there to comfort and protect her. They stayed in that moment for a little while, He wanted to make sure she was confident in herself and God.

"I love you princess, and so does God. He provides a way for us. He will have his way and plans for this child." Theo said, giving another comforting smile.

"Yeah," Ela said, smiling at him.

34

Growing Stronger, Physically and Spiritually

Two months have passed, Theo is home from the hospital, his ribs have healed but is still on crutches for his leg. I am now four months pregnant. The morning sickness stopped last week. Theo doesn't want to know the gender of the baby till we have it.

I got out of bed and got ready. Theo has been sleeping on the couch in the living room, as it is hard for him to go up the stairs. I went down stairs and saw Theo reading his Bible, with his broken leg propped up.

"Good morning" I said, making my way to him.

"Good morning, beautiful," Theo said, looking up from his Bible.

"What have you got planned today?" Theo asked, putting his Bible on the coffee table.

"I don't know yet. Maybe hang out in the garden. Maybe help Grandma and the maid fix up the nursery." I said, sitting beside him.

"This isn't exactly fair, I should be the one fixing up the nursery, but instead I am stuck down here, with this cast." Theo said, running his hand through his hair.

"Yeah, but God had a plan from the beginning. He knew what he was doing, he blessed you by keeping you alive, and probably by slowing you down, he managed to get you closer to him" I said.

"I know, I love you, my lady" Theo said, taking my hand and kissing the back of it.

"I love you too," I said.

We did a morning devotional and then I went upstairs, as Theo turned the laptop on and started on his CEO work. I went to the guest bedroom that we are turning into a nursery. I walked in and saw they were putting up the crib. It was a beautiful birch wood crib. The room was decorated in God's creations (animals). The walls painted a beautiful cyan color.

"Anything I can help with?' I asked.

"Nope nope, you go enjoy some time with Theo, We got this" Edna said, guiding me out of the room.

I giggled and went back down stairs. I got a Christian book and started to read. I noticed Theo watching me every so often. He would quickly turn back to his work, when I tried to look at him. I finished the book and looked at my phone, it was noon.

I got up and stretched, went to the kitchen and started to cook. I cooked steak and potatoes. For dessert, I made cheesecake bites. Theo went into the dining room and sat down at the table. I placed our food on the table. Theo put his crutches out of the way. I went to go get Edna and the maid. We came back down and blessed the food.

"Dear heavenly father, we want to thank you for this day. Lord, we pray that you bless this food in the nourishment of our body and bodies for your service. We thank you Lord for our family." Theo blessed the food.

We began eating the food. Once we were done, I gathered all the dishes and put them in the sink. I was about to clean them when the maid stopped me and told me to go sit down. They were protecting me, but I think they are being a little over protective, I am only four months at this time.

Theo and I went to watch a Christian show. The show lasted for an hour and a half. Theo wanted to go out to the garden, so we got the wheelchair from the closet and he sat in it. I pushed him out into the garden. We enjoyed being surrounded by God's creation. We stayed there till it was time to go to bed.

35

It's Time

Months have passed, Theo was healed from all broken bones. Ela is now thirty seven weeks pregnant. Theo was so proud of her, for getting over the past and protecting the child growing in her. He noticed she was uncomfortable most of the night. She woke up like she was in pain.

"Princess? Are you ok?" Theo asked.

"Yeah, I think it is just the Braxton-Hicks again. I have had them since I was thirty two weeks pregnant. I am fine" Ela said.

"I don't know, you look like you are more uncomfortable than before." Theo said, helping her out of bed.

"I am fine. Don't worry," Ela said.

They got ready and went down stairs. When they got into the living room, Edna saw them and a face of realization hit her. She walked to Ela and held her hands.

"Dear, don't mistake your labor pains for braxton hicks. You have all the signs of labor. Please go to the hospital and have my great grandchild." Edna said.

"Okay, we can go to the hospital again to just see if I am actually in labor" Ela said, As Theo grabbed the stuff and headed to the car.

Theo and Ela made their way to the hospital. Some time later, they arrived. A nurse guided them into a room and checked Ela to see if she was in labor. The nurse smiled and turned to them.

"Mrs. Ambrose, you are in labor, I will go get the doctor. Would you like an epidural for the pain?" The nurse said.

"Yes, please." Ela said.

Fifteen minutes later, the nurse came back with the epidural. Ela took the epidural and laid back down. The doctor came in thirty minutes later. They moved Ela and Theo to a labor and delivery room.

"You two ready to meet your precious little miracle?" The doctor said,

"Yep, you got this, God is with you and he has made you strong." Theo said, kissing Ela's head.

The labor and giving birth took two hours. Ela was exhausted but happy. The doctor let her hold their newborn baby boy. They moved them all to a recovery room. Once they were in the room, the doctor checked all vitals of Ela and the baby.

"What are you gonna name this little one?" The doctor asked.

"Axel" Theo said

"Meaning father of peace, nice" The doctor said.

"Here you go Mr. Ambrose, give your wife some rest" The doctor said, handing the baby to Theo.

Theo took baby Axel and sat on the couch holding him in his arms. Ela started to doze off to sleep. Theo watched Axel in his arms. He felt overjoyed and grateful to be holding his own child in his arms.

'Lord, thank you so much for this miracle and incredible opportunity. I pray over Ela that you heal her and give her strength. I pray over this little one in my arms, I give him to you Lord. I pray that he can please you, when he gets older. Lord, help us through these new times. We are both ecstatic for this little miracle you have given us. Thank you so much Lord, protect us all. In your holy name I pray amen'

Theo finished praying and put baby Axel in the bassinet the hospital had in the room. Theo took a picture on his phone and sent it to Liam and Edna. He sat in the chair beside Ela's bed. He held her hand as she slept.

"Good job, princess, you did well," Theo said, kissing her hand.

Theo moved the bassinet closer to the both of them. Edna came to the hospital thirty minutes later. She came into the room. Theo put his finger in a shush motion and pointed towards Ela sleeping.

"Oh, such a precious little thing. I am so proud of the both of you. May God use your family for his will." Edna whispered, looking at baby Axel.

"The maid is bringing up a fruit basket for you two, Make sure she eats some of it to get her strength back up" Edna Whispered to Theo.

Edna placed the basket on one of the hospital tables. She hugged her grandson and hugged Ela, who was still sleeping. Theo said goodbye to her and checked on Axel. Axel started to try to fuss. Theo picked him up and changed his diaper. He held Axel in his arms till he calmed down.

Axel went back to sleep, so Theo put him back in the bassinet. The nurse came in then, checked on Ela's vitals. Ela woke up then. The nurse finished and Axel started to cry again.

"Hand him here, it is time to feed him again." Ela said

Theo handed Axel to Ela and she began to breastfeed him. Theo stayed close to Ela and Axel. He adored watching over them with care. He was so proud of Ela. Ela finished feeding Axel and burped him. He went back to sleep after that.

"Here, he can go back to the bassinet now" Ela said, handing Theo the baby.

"Okay" Theo said, taking Axel and putting him back in the bassinet.

They spent the rest of the day taking care of Axel, reading the Bible and talking to God. Ela and Theo both adored Axel. They thanked God every chance they could get. The night was a new experience for them. They made it through. Ela and Axel Got discharged the day after.

A few months went by, all the animals at the center were all adopted, and Ela had more animals surrendered to the center. It took time for the both of them to adjust to having Axel, but they enjoyed every moment of it.

Epilogue

I woke up at 5:00 A.M. I got ready for the day and went to the nursery. Axel was awake in the crib. I turned the lights on and picked him up out of the crib. I took him to the changing table.

"Good morning, my little one. Let's get you changed and ready for the day." I said.

I changed his diaper and clothes. He turned one year old today. We went downstairs and I put him in his high chair. The maid put all the food on the table. I fixed Axel's bottle and set it on the table. I smashed some bananas on his plate and added some of my eggs. I blessed all of the food and started to feed him and myself.

"Good morning" Theo said, coming into the kitchen and giving both me and Axel a kiss on the head.

"What do we have planned today?" Theo asked, sitting in his spot at the table.

"Go to church, then Avery and Liam want to take the kids to the park for a picnic." I said, giving Axel a bite of eggs, as Edna came to sit at the table.

"Seems like a fun and eventful day" Theo said, taking a bite of bacon.

"Yep" I said.

We finished breakfast and finished getting ready for church. I wore a yellow sun dress with white wedge heels. Axel wore a blue baby button down shirt with baby khaki shorts, with brown sandals. Theo wore a black tux, with his Sunday shoes.

"Okay, Axel, let's go put you in your car seat." I said, putting him in the car seat, which was in the Jeep.

"You ready to go, my queen" Theo said, putting all the stuff in the trunk.

"Yep" I said, getting into the passenger seat.

Edna stayed in the backseat with Axel, as Theo drove us to church. We arrived and got out. I grabbed Axel out of his car seat. Theo grabbed the diaper bag and Bibles. We went inside and sat beside Avery and Liam.

The church service started and we worshiped and listened to the sermon. The sermon was on the last days. We were dismissed at twelve thirty and we left the church. We met Avery and Liam at the park.

Liam was setting up the playpen beside the table. Avery put Bella in the play pen with a stuffed animal. I put Axel in there with Bella as he was learning to crawl. We blessed our food and began eating.

"I can't believe she is growing so fast." Theo said, looking at the babies in the playpen.

"I know, I can't believe she is already two years old and walking." Liam said.

"It went by really quickly. She was a tiny little baby and now she is our little two year old." Avery said, handing a bite of sandwich to Bella.

I got Axel out as he was getting fussy. Liam got the bottle and baby baby food out of the diaper bag. He started to feed Axel as I held him and ate my food. Axel was a happy baby, always smiling and laughing. The only time he fussed was when he was hungry or needed his diaper changed. We thank God every day for everything that he has done for us. We are raising Axel by God's ways and by reading Bible stories to him. We are so blessed with this incredible life journey. God has blessed us so much, from beginning to end.

About the Author

Elisha White is an author, tik toker, gamer, youtuber, Christian and founder of The Saved Coop. She loves to spend her free time playing video games, reading/writing books, reading the bible or watching youtube with her cat. Her favorite bible verse is Jeremiah 29:11. She loves her church and her family, even when they don't see eye to eye. She got saved in January 2023. She does daily bible studies morning and night.